Tommy

Michael D. Goldsmith

Copyright © 2022 Michael D. Goldsmith

All rights reserved.

DEDICATION

I dedicate this book to my Father. Wayne Eldon Goldsmith. He died before my first book came out.

I pray he is able to read my works in heaven where he is now. One day shortly before his passing, he had told my mom somehow his radio had been turned to a "preacher. He told her he had received Christ as his Savior. Dad, This ones for you.

ACKNOWLEDGEMENT

I would like to thank My Lord and Savior Jesus Christ for saving me. Without him in my life nothing like this would have happened.

Contents

DEDICATION III
ACKNOWLEDGEMENT IV
1. BEGINNING 1
2. BACK TO SCHOOL 8
3. LEADER OF THE "PACK." 11
4. THE NEW PACK 17
5. THE DRAFT 25
6. TRAINING CAMP 30
7. DINNER WITH KATE AND JON 36
8. THE START OF SOMETHING BIG 43
9. THE FUN STARTS 48
10. SEASON TWO OF THE TOMMY AND GREGG SHOW 58
11. ADVENTURE ON THE FLIGHT BACK 67
12. THE GREGG AND TOMMY SHOW CONTINUES 77
13. THE LAST SEASON 79
14. THEY MEET IN MINNESOTA, AGAIN! 82
15. THAT FINAL SEASON 89
16. THE SEASON GETS TOUGH 93
17. SUPERBOWL HERE WE COME 111
EPILOGUE 118

1. BEGINNING

Super Bowl Sunday. Wide receiver – Tommy Richardson had just played his last game with the great Herman McBrien. Minnesota had just won its first Superbowl. Tommy was standing beside Herman at the podium. The reporters were asking them all sorts of questions. Patricia Johnson asked Tommy a question that she really was not expecting the in-depth answer she would receive. "Tommy, I understand you and Herman go way back. Can you tell me how you guys met? What is your history?

Tommy smiled. "How much time do you have? It all started before Herman was born. You see, I met his parents first. Here's how it played out."

The morning had started like many others since I had been sick. I was a 10-year-old boy who had been an adventuress, to say the least. But for the last several months, I had been totally wiped out. My mother took me to Doctor Johnson, my pediatrician. Dr. Johnson had run a myriad of tests to figure out what was wrong. He was suspicious, so he sent me to Dr. Jonsmith for a second opinion.

That morning the phone rang. "Hello, this is Janice. Can I help you?"

"Janice, this is Dr. Johnson's office. The test results are in. We would like you to come in today if you could?" The kind voice on the other end of the line asked.

"What time would be good?" My mom asked.

"How about one o'clock?" That was the response.

Tommy

You see, I had leukemia. And I was about to have my first divine appointment. Eli's McBriens wife Jill would save my life." He and Herman would smile and step down off the podium with that. The friendship would last a lifetime. Now for the rest of the story.

- * -

The Father looked at Peter. "Pete, what your about to see here is one example of how I can use something that would destroy a family and build something great out of it. They think they will have a chance to meet with one of my greatest servants. What they are about to experience is what can happen from one of my divine appointments." The Father said.

- * -

As Janice and Tommy walked in, they were met by a male nurse. "Tommy, let me take you over to the computer. We have a baseball game on there I think you would find really great" Smiling, Tommy went over to the computer game to play with the male nurse.

Janice walked into the doctor's inner office to hear the news. "Mrs. Richardson, I am not going to beat around the bush with this. Tommy has a severe form of leukemia; the only thing that can save him is a bone marrow transplant. The problem is Tommy has an extremely rare blood type - AB negative. Unless we find a transplant, he will die."

Janice turned white. The tears started to come like a flood in the spring after huge snowfalls all winter. She nodded and got up, and walked out of the room. Her mind was racing, trying to grasp what had just happened. She started asking one question that millions of parents had asked before. "Why God, Why?"

- * -

Peter looked at the Father and asked the same question. "Father, why? Why would you put her through this?

The Father just had a few words for Peter. "Stand back and watch me work." Turned and walked away, looked at Jesus, his Son, as the tears were coming down his face.

Tommy

_ * _

Janice and Tommy Richardson walked out of the doctor's office. Janice was in tears but tried desperately to hide them from her son Tommy. She had lost her husband the year before and had just found out her son Tommy had leukemia. She knew she had to handle this in the most gentle way possible. How does one tell a 10-year-old that unless they can find a marrow donor in the next few months, he will die? Her heart was heavy. She smiled and said. "Tommy, I think we need to go to a baseball game today. LA is playing St. Louis, and your hero Eli McBrien is pitching. How would you like to do that?"

"Mom, that would be great, but can we get tickets?" The young boy answered.

Janice smiled and said. "Let's do it." They got to the stadium. They asked to get tickets and ended up with the nosebleed section of the outfield. They turned, and Dr. Johnson was standing right behind them. "Here, I'll trade you!" he said.

Tommy's eyes got big as saucers. The excitement could be seen rising in his facial expressions. "Please trade with him, mom, PLEASE!?"

Janice looked over at the good Doctor. He winked at her. She smiled and said. "Doctor Johnson, I don't know how to thank you. These seats are wonderful. Just above L.A.s dugout. I can't thank you enough."

_ * _

The Father of all mankind looked over at Peter. "Pete, what you're about to see most people would call a miracle; to me, it's what I do every day. This is gonna be fun. When they asked why the man was born blind, My Son set them straight. It was done for My Glory. For the rest of his years, man could see on earth and still see here in heaven. It shall also be for Tommy. Watch me work."

_ * _

Eli McBrien. That day would be magic for Tommy. He would get all the food and drinks he could handle and have a close look at the greatest pitcher ever.

Eli looked up to the stadium and caught Tommy's eye. When he got back to the dugout, he motioned to his bat boy and had him take a signed ball up to Tommy.

When the bat boy found Tommy and gave him the ball, Tommy was ecstatic. Soon, the game was over, and it was time to go home. That night was not a good one for Tommy. He was so sick. But the next morning was better.

Janice looked at Tommy. "Young man, I think this morning we have to go out to breakfast.

Tommy looked at his mom and asked a question that would force her to draw on every bit of strength that she had. "Mommy, how sick am I really? Am I going to die?"

With a tear in her eye and emotion in her voice, Janice told the young lad the truth. It was him knowing the truth that would set him free.

Janice then stepped back from Tommy. Tommy, I think it's time we went to breakfast at Jerry's on the beach. I don't know why, but I feel maybe God is sending us there this morning."

As they arrived at Jerry's at 10 a.m., they noticed a real fancy car in the parking lot. Tommy looked at his mom and said. "Whoever owns that has to have a lot of money."

They walked inside and sat near a window overlooking the ocean. Tommy looked over and saw Eli McBrien and his wife, Jill. The excitement on his face was without measure. "Mom, can I get his autograph? Please, please, please?"

Janice went inside her purse and found a small notebook handed to Tommy, who walked up to Eli's table. The boy said, in somewhat of a weak voice, "Mr. McBrien, my name is Tommy. You see, Mr. McBrien, I will not be here much longer. Could you make it out to my mom? I would like her to have something special to remember me by."

Eli looked at his mom, then at Jill. "Tommy, what's your mom's name?"

Tommy looked at his mom. "Janice."

Eli excused himself and walked to the other side of the restaurant where Janice was sitting. "Janice, what's wrong with Tommy?"

Tommy has a rare form of leukemia. There is only one bone marrow transplant in a million that will work. He has AB-negative blood."

Eli excused himself, walked over to his bride, and gave Jill a kiss on the cheek. "Hun, you have AB-negative blood, don't you?" he asked.

Jill got a puzzled look on her face. "Yes, why?"

"Go talk to Tommy's mom for a moment," he asked ever so sweetly.

_ * _

"Pete, do you see how in this instance, all things will work for the good, and does this help you understand divine appointments?" Then the Father continued. This may help you understand why I do what I do."

Pete answered," Yes, Father, I think I do understand."

_ * _

Jill walked over to Janice, "What is wrong with Tommy?"

Janice had tears running down her cheek as she told Jill what the problem was. Jill looked at Janice and started crying. "I had a miscarriage last month. We lost a little girl. Why don't I get checked? If my marrow is a match, then we can use it."

All Janice could say was, "Thank you!"

Before Jill and Eli arrived back at their condo, Jill's phone rang. "This is Jill. Yes…aha…we'll be there, two o'clock. That will be fine."

Eli, with a very questioning look on his face, asked, "What was that about?"

"I have an appointment to check my bone marrow, to see if I am a match for Tommy," was the sweet answer his beautiful bride gave.

_ * _

Pete looked to Father. "Father, am I seeing another miracle here?"

The Father chuckled. "Pete, there are no miracles with me. This is what I do every day."

_ * _

At 2:00 p.m. sharp, Jill and Eli arrived at the clinic for the test. Eli walked in with Jill, and they sat down and waited. The receptionist came out and said, "Jill McBrien." Eli started to get up to go with her. "Sorry, Mr. McBrien, but you must sit here," the nurse told Eli in a very stern voice.

Jill went into the examining room. She was told to lie on her stomach. They inserted a needle into her. There was some pain, but not a great deal. After a small sample of marrow was pulled, she was told she could get up and leave. The nurse told her she would be notified if there was a match. She was also told not to get her hopes up, as the boy was an exceedingly rare case.

Two weeks went by, and Eli had his first game as a coach. His team won big time. Jamaal got two home runs, and both Sammy and Thaddeus got their first wins.

Jill was shopping with Corrine when her cell went off. "Hi, this is Jill."

The nurse on the other end responded, "Jill, this is Helen Johnson from Park Hill Clinic. You're a match. Are you still willing to donate?"

"Yes, of course! When?" was Jill's immediate response.

"Tomorrow at six in the morning. Can you check in tonight?"

"Of course!"

Jill hung up and called Eli. "Hun, I am a match! I AM A MATCH!"

The answer from Eli was quick. "Sweetheart, when do you donate?"

His greatest gift answered ever so sweetly. "I have to check in tonight, and they pull the marrow in the morning. I go home the same day."

That night Eli took his beautiful bride to a great restaurant then to the hospital.

As Jill slept, Eli walked the hall. He walked past little Tommy's room. His mom was beside the bed. Eli could tell that she was hurting.

Eli stepped into the room ever so quietly. He put his hand on Tommy's mom's shoulder and asked if he could pray for her.

Through her tears, she smiled at Eli and said, "Please do."

Eli prayed. "Father, I know you have this under control. Give Janice the peace that passes understanding. Give little Tommy many more years to serve you. I ask these things in Jesus's name." He smiled, touched her shoulder, left the room, and walked to Jill's. Eli slept in the chair beside Jill's bed. He wanted to take Jill home in the morning after the procedure.

Morning came quickly. The nurse came in, and they pushed Eli out of the way to get Jill to the procedure room. The whole process would be a huge success. Tommy would live to be a huge success on the football field. His legend would be so great stories would be written about him for many years to come. He would play college ball at Nebraska and fifteen years as a pro, first with Dallas, then with Minnesota. He would be a huge factor in teaching young kids the value of never, ever giving up.

2. BACK TO SCHOOL

Tommy, the next Monday, would head back to school. His friends were ecstatic. His 4th-grade teacher, Mrs. Jones, would have a party for him. They put signs up saying welcome back all over the school. When Tommy walked in, his smile was as wide as a mile. His excitement knew no bounds. His energy level was through the roof. He was hopping up and down the halls.

- * -

The Father smiled at Peter. "Pete, I am so excited about what is going to become of Tommy. Tommy Richardson will be a household name in the years to come. I will get the credit for everything he accomplishes in his life. This is going to be so much fun."

The first afternoon, Mrs. Jones had the children outside for Phys. Ed. She decided to have the children run a 50-meter race. She would have Tommy not race as she was concerned about his health. "Mrs. Jones, please let me run. I have not been able to for such a long time. Just let me try?"

Mrs. Jones smiled. "Okay, young man, line up with your fellow runners." After they lined up, she looked at them and said. "Ready, set, go!!!" They were off. Tommy ran so fast no one else was within 15 yards when he crossed the finish line.

- * -

The Father looked over at Pete. "Pete, what do you think of this young lad who is going to be a great servant of mine. Stuff like this really excites me." The Father said with a huge smile.

_ * _

Tommy's mom Janet was on the sidelines watching her son run. At first, she was a bit apprehensive about letting him run. When she saw him blow down the track, her jaw dropped wide open. She knew that she was seeing nothing short of a miracle happen in her son. She was not sure just how to handle what was going on. But she did understand that God the Father through his Son Jesus by his Holy Spirit was at work in her boy. She looked up to heaven. "Father, what do you have in store for this young boy that you have given me? What are you going to do with Tommy?

_ * _

"Pete, Janet is about to learn that when I do something, I do it big. What she is about to find out is this. I have created her son to accomplish great things for my purpose. I decide when people are born and when they die. I am the only one with that right. I have big plans for Tommy. Stay tuned. This is gonna be a fun ride."

_ * _

Mrs. Jones stood in front of her class. She told the class to quiet down. "Tommy, I have been told that you had a bone marrow transplant. I was also told that the way you met your donor was a miracle. Would you like to tell the class about it?"

Tommy would spend the next hour telling the class about Jill McBrien and how the Lord brought them together. As he talked, the class asked more and more questions. All Tommy could do was answer the best he could. But the more questions he answered, the more excited he became. "It's like this. I felt like sleeping all the time. I could almost see my body dying. Then right after the surgery, I was starving. I felt like running up and down the hallway. You guys need to really understand this. Life is exciting. Life feels great. You know what. I feel like something else great will happen to me because of Eli and Jill

McBrien. I don't know what? But I really feel like something else great is going to happen."

The next couple of years would pass quickly. Tommy would soon find himself playing football in middle school. On his first day on the field, Coach Wolf would send Tommy out on a long pass. He would catch it without a problem. In his first game, it happened time and again. Tommy would score three touchdowns in his first, middle school game. This would be the beginning of what would be a great football career. But he would also become the "leader of the pack."

3. LEADER OF THE "PACK."

The Father looked over at Peter. "I think it's time we put Thumbnail to work on another case. We have got to get Tommy through these years. The temptation will be to succumb to what the world has to offer. I did not put him together with Eli and Jill to save his life for him not to follow me all of his life."

Instantly, Thumbnail was front and center. The Great I Am looked at Thumbnail and smiled. "Little one, you know what I want you to do with Tommy."

Thumbnail, who loved to serve the Father, had only one thing to say. "Father, this young man has a great destiny ahead of him. Let's get him there."

_ * _

As Tommy walked into his middle school, he found a crowd of his fellow students gathering around him. Everyone, especially the girls, seemed to hang on to every word he said. He would walk down the hall, and the crowd would follow him. He felt pride in what he had just accomplished. He knew his great ability on the football field put him in the situation. He was feeling pride in himself. He would soon learn pride comes before destruction. The next game would prove to be a disaster for him. He would drop three passes in the endzone. He seemed to have to ball zeroed in, then it would move, and he would miss it. He could almost hear little giggles on every play.

_ * _

Thumbnail found himself in the presence of God the Father. Jesus was sitting beside His Father on his throne. The Father looked down on Thumbnail. "I hope you enjoyed yourself. Now it's time to build him back up to where we need him. He will be the leader of the pack. I want you to speak to him today. Let him know where his greatness comes from. After all, I did create him."

Thumbnail, as he had done with Eli many times before, hovered next to Tommy's ear. "Tommy, God the Father through His Son by His Spirit set up your bone marrow transplant. Now it's time you give him credit for all that He has created you to be. Tonight, at practice, you will catch every pass. Your coach will trust you to play well in your next game. You will become the star that The Father has created you to be. You will be the star in your next game. When the students gather around you, The Father would like you to give him credit for your greatness. The more credit you give him, the greater player you will become. The Father has big plans for you."

_ * _

That night at practice, it was like his hands had glue on them. He would seem to have the ball going over his head, and a burst of speed that he did not even know he had in him would put him right under the ball. His coach scratched his head. Thumbnail hovered right at the coaches' ear. "Trust him." That was what Thumbnail would say to him.

The next game was truly blessed. He caught every ball. Scored 4 touchdowns. When he walked into school, it was once again Monday; he was the pack leader. But this time would be different. He had a crowd around him. He stepped up on a step and began to speak. "Hey guys, I appreciate your attention. But the attention really needs to go to our Lord Jesus Christ. He told a parable one time about guys with talents. My talents are a gift from God himself. He brought a lady into my life who donated bone marrow to cure leukemia. I will dedicate whatever talents I am given to his kingdom and his glory. So, let's keep that in mind whenever we accomplish something great. One other thing, I am part of a team. Do you realize the team effort that went into the win? I am not the sole reason those touchdowns were scored. Every member of the team had their part. The offence, the defence, special teams all had a part in the whole. The only one who gets all of the credit is God the Father through His Son Jesus by His Holy Spirit."

Tommy turned and walked up the steps to his first class of the day.

At lunchtime, Tommy was walking down the hall. Jim Jordon, his coach, walked up behind him and tapped him on the shoulder. "Tommy, what you did this morning took a lot of self-discipline. With the game you had the other night, it would have been easy for anyone to really start bragging. But you are laying it out as a team effort really kept the rest of the team on board. Jimmy knows all he has to do is get that ball close to you, and you make him look really good."

Tommy looked at his coach. "Coach, what I said is really true. If one of our linemen misses a block, Jimmy does not get the pass off, and I don't score. If the passing game is not set up by the running game, I would never get open. Coach. God, our Father, has a mission for me to accomplish. But I can't do it alone. I know this. Football is going to be a huge part of it. Baseball can be controlled by a pitcher if he has a hot day. 11 men must work like a well-oiled machine to make things happen on a football field. When that happens, championships are won."

Jim put his hand on Tommy's shoulder. "Tommy, you have wisdom beyond your years. I feel you're destined for some great things in your life. But know this. You are created to lead. Lead by example, but also lead by what you say. You have you. Let's do this. Three high school years ahead of you. You also have college. Let's do this for all the other

After practice, Tommy walked home by himself. He was thinking about everything his coach had said to him that day. "How am I supposed to be an example to all the kids in school? I don't even know myself well enough yet to be that kind of great leader."

Thumbnail was hovering just above his head, listening to every thought he thought. He spoke directly into Tommy's ear. "Tommy, you gave the glory to God when you spoke to the students today. God has created you for such a time as this. He is going to accomplish some real greatness with you. But he has also created you to lead his people. So, lead them you must. "

Thoughts were flooding Tommy's mind. "I am a kid; how is God going to use me to lead his people."

Thumbnail, hearing his thoughts, said to him. "God the Father used David at a young age. He used Joseph at a young age as well. Don't sell yourself short. The Father uses those who are sold out to him. If you keep your eyes on the Father through the Son by His Holy

Spirit, he will use you in ways that will blow people away. When he sent you and your mom to the restaurant to meet Eli and Jill, he knew that it would save your life. He created you to lead his people. Don't take this whole thing lightly. You are created to lead. Just remember this. You must always stay humble."

From that time on, he was a humble hero at the school of the Master in his hometown. After practice, he always led the team in prayer. In his senior year, they were playing San Diego central. With 10 seconds left, John Smith, the cornerback who made all the receivers from all the other teams look like mere puppets as he intercepted a pass after pass, was given the job of covering Tommy. Tommy smiled at him as they were lined up against each other with the mere 10 seconds left to play. With a quick juke, Tommy had him faked out of his shoes. Slim Johnson, his quarterback, hit him right in the hands, and he was in the endzone for the win. He walked up to John after the play. Smiled and shrugged his shoulders and winked. They were headed to state.

Tommy would score a total of 7 touchdowns in the state tournament. The University of California had been watching him since his sophomore year. They had touched base with his parents but not with him. Right after the state final was won, the coaches for California state would come knocking on his door. The recruiting process would be a lot of fun for Tommy. His mind, however, kept going back to the morning, eating breakfast and getting Eli McBriens autograph. His life would change forever.

The recruiters from California were all over him. They wanted this home state boy staying in his home state. The first day he would walk into the locker room of state, trying to decide if this is where he wanted to be or not, he would meet Reese. Reese was a tight end. Tommy was a quick wide receiver. As they talked, Reese was more than cordial. But Tommy was not used to such warmth and love coming from someone he did not know.

Reese would walk up to his coach. "Coach, this kid, Tommy, has to come here. There is something about him that is a cut above. I think I could share what you guys have taught me about football. I see a great friendship here. He just does not know it yet."

Coach Wolf chuckled. "So, you think you two could be my dynamic duo? Do you think you could drive the secondaries of the opposition nuts trying to cover you?"

Tommy looked at his potential coach. "Think? I know we could accomplish that. I have seen Reese play. You put the two of us together, and you will win many games. Trust me!"

The coach smiled. "Tommy, it's time to see how good you really are?" He picked up the phone and called in two of his best cornerbacks. Keith Johnson, and Layle Mullenix. As they walked into his office, the coach shut the door. "Gentlemen, Tommy Richardson is getting dressed for a little workout. I am going to put you on him with double coverage. He made those poor guys trying to cover him in the state finals look like grade-schoolers. You will not let him get open. Is that understood?"

The two young men answered in unison." Yes, sir!"

_ * _

The Father looked over at Peter. "You see those two young men; I have given them some great talent to be able to cover receivers. They are about to get faked out of their jockstraps. Just watch this. Tommy is still on the earth for a reason. No one will stop him."

Peter smiled, knowing that what the Father had in mind would soon be revealed.

_ * _

The 4 young gentlemen and the coaches walked out onto the field. Coach Wolf had the Tommy line up, and the two corners line up opposite him. Joe Smith, his quarterback, called the signals. The ball was snapped. Tommy faked the two corners out, caught the ball, and headed back to the coach. "What you think, coach?" Tommy asked.

Coach Wolf looked at Tommy and said." A young man once is a fluke; let's see it again." That afternoon Tommy would run 10 routes. The same result would happen each time. On the 11th, they were able to keep Tommy covered. "Tommy, we would love to have you here playing football with us. What do you say?" Coach Wolf asked him."

Tommy looked at his mom, standing on the field watching her son.

She smiled and nodded. Tommy looked at the coach and said. "I think this is where I want to play ball. It is close enough that my mom will get to the games. And I think this is really going to open doors for what God the Father wants me to accomplish in my life."

The coach did a double-take. Being a believer himself, he knew that Tommy was right. He also knew he would have to support what this young man would do on and off the field. He could see that Tommy would be the Leader of the Pack for years to come. He looked at Tommy and said. "Tommy, there are several Christian organizations on campus. When you get here next year, I will make sure you are put in contact with each of them."

Tommy smiled.

The next Monday, he walked into school. His classmates wanted to know all about what happened at California State. Tommy smiled as he told them about the whole thing. He became the most excited about telling them about all the Christian organizations on campus. He knew that they had only 7 months together as a class at the high school. He knew that for the next 7 months, God the Father had placed him there to lead them to where he needed them to be. He had been a leader on campus for years. He knew that he had to use the left time to see more kids understand that Jesus the Christ had come to save them. He also knew that he had to knock out top grades to be the pack leader.

As the year went on, Tommy would get used to getting in touch with kids. He would help them with their math and English. He would pray with his fellow students to receive Christ into their lives. He would truly be the Leader of the Pack. But the year came to an end ever so quickly. The students would all go their separate ways. Tommy would find himself becoming part of the pack at California State.

4. THE NEW PACK

That summer would be magic. He would spend his days at the beach with his classmates, the nights at different venues where the Gospel of Christ was being preached. June and July passed quickly. Soon August would be upon him, and he would walk onto the Cal. State campus for the dreaded two-a-days. High School ball was a piece of cake compared to what he was experiencing in this situation. He would experience pain like he had not in the past. He knew, however, that to reach the top, one had to pay the price and pay the price he would.

Their first game was against the Cowboys of Houston state. Tommy's quickness would prove too much for the Cowboys as his quarterback, Chet Thomas would hit him repeatedly with pinpoint accuracy. He would score 3 touchdowns. Not to mention all the heroics he would display with some of his catches. When he would walk onto campus Monday, he thought his experience would be pretty much the same as in High School.

When he walked onto campus Monday, he could almost hear the "thud." No one was there. No girls were fawning over him. His platform was gone. He would look to heaven and ask the Father one question through the Son by the Spirit. "Now what, Father. How do I function here? How do I use my position to reach those around me?"

- * -

The Father looked at Peter and smiled. "Pete, watch the character development that Tommy is about to go through. Granted, he is a great football player, and he is sold out to me, but he is about to learn what it means to be just a body on campus. Athletic prowess in High School is one thing; it's not that big of a deal in college. Everyone is on campus for the same reason. To get an education. Sports are considered entertainment, like going to concerts, plays, or even dances. Not much more than that. He does not see what I have planned for him after college. I have plans for that boy in my purpose. He will be used to touching kids in a way that will blow people's minds. Just watch and see."

- * -

Tommy walked up to the campus chaplain to ask him a question. The chaplain John Kincaid rose from his desk to meet Tommy at his door. Tommy shook his hand, walked with him to his desk, and sat in the chair at one side of his desk that Josh motioned him to. "John, I thought being a great football player would open doors for me to be able to share what Christ has done for me. When I walked on campus Monday, it was not there. I was not noticed as I walked down the hall. I certainly am not the hero here that I was in high school." Tommy said.

John sat on the corner of his desk. "Tommy, what is your major?" John asked.

"Physics." Was Tommy's answer.
"What are you going to do with that?" John asked.
"I want to work in the nuclear industry," Tommy said.

"Pretty tough subject, but here's the deal. Every student here has a goal. That goal is to be the best they can be in any field that they go into. In high school, sports were, in large part, the school's identity. It's not here. It's entertainment. It's a break from the school's pressure on all its students. It has nothing to do with academics. I hope that helps you understand. Everyone here is looking to be the best in their field." John stated.

"So, let me get this straight. The coaches worked hard to get me to come here. They did that so I could be an entertainer for my fellow students?"

John smiled, "Not entirely, you see if the school's football team does well, the team gets the attention of the big donors who attended here in the past. You see, it's not the students here now who get excited about a football game. It's the alumni. They want bragging rights at their country clubs. Let's say that you have two guys playing golf. One is from here, the other from Notre Dame. Let's say we are playing them in a bowl game. That game is exciting for a few weeks here, but it gives bragging rights all year on the golf course.

Now let's say you are as outspoken about Christ as I think you will be with your 4 years here. You have the same two guys on the golf course. Here, the one brings up the point that you are sold out to Christ and work with kids off-campus. Now compare that to an athlete who is not a great guy. Maybe rapes a young lady on campus. Or who is the Father of a child out of wedlock? One player gives the school a black eye. The other brings a radiance to the school. It's that radiance that the school is looking for in its recruitment of players. You bring Glory to the Father through the Son by the Spirit, and you will bask in His glory." John stated authoritatively.

Tommy smiled slightly. He looked at the chaplain. "That explains a lot to me about why I am still on this earth." He said.

"What do you mean?" John asked.

"John, when I was a young boy, I had leukemia; unless I received a bone marrow transplant, I would die. My mom felt the nudge to take me to breakfast at a very upscale restaurant. When we arrived there, I saw a great-looking car. It turned out to belong to Eli McBrien. To make a long story short, Jill, his wife, donated bone marrow so I could live. You see, John, I have a rare blood type. Very few people have this type. Jill did. I am alive because God the Father brought us together through His Son by His Spirit. I have an obligation to be a vehicle to share Jesus with the world. The Father has placed me here to share his love. He is using football to do it."

John smiled. "Tommy, I think we need to be reaching out in a bigger way. Let's see what the next few games hold for you. You need to get active with a Christian Ministry here on campus. I can see the Father using you in some great outreaches."

The next few games were tremendous. Monday morning, Tommy walked onto campus. Suddenly, a couple of students came up to him. "Aren't you Tommy Richardson, the new wide receiver?" They asked.

"Yup, that's me. What can I do for you?" Tommy asked.
"That was a great game!" His fellow students said. Then they turned and walked away.

Tommy looked to heaven. "Okay, Father, I get it; just because I can catch a football, I am not a hero. I am a guy who can catch a football. How do I use that to accomplish your greatness here on campus? How do I use that for your kingdom?" He turned to walk down the hall. He stopped and looked up to a 12 ft. tall Gabriel. "Who are you?" He asked.

"Young man, I have a message directly from the Father for you. You need not worry about how the Father will use you in any situation. You need to worry about using the gifts the Father has given you for his glory. When you do that, he will open doors of ministry for you that will blow your mind. When that happens, you will see the lives changed of those he brings to you. Your job is not to worry. Your job is to do. The Father is not worried about your importance; the Father will use you, don't worry about your importance but the ones he brings across your path. Their eternity depends on you being willing to share what the Father has done through His Son by His Spirit giving you back your life. Don't worry, just do what the Father has for you to do. By the way, my name is Gabriel."

Tommy looked away and back. Gabriel was gone. He looked up and down the hall; there were students everywhere, but there was No Gabriel anywhere. As he walked down the hallway, he saw an altercation. Two students were yelling at each other. Standing 6'4", he could have quite an imposing figure. He stepped in between the two people. One of the students was about to throw a punch at Tommy. "I would not do that if I were you. I think I could probably break you in half, but I would let the campus police take care of this situation instead of myself. I must ask you two one question. Do you know Jesus Christ?"

"What does that have to do with this?" Jack Brown, one of the two, asked?"

Tommy chuckled. "Jesus said." As you have done it onto the least of these, my brothers, you have done it onto me."

Harry, the other student, spoke up. "So, if I smack this idiot, I am smacking Jesus?"

Tommy smiled. "Pretty much, we are called to be of help to our brother and sister when we can. Not to get angry and knock each other around."

Jack looked at Tommy and asked. "What's your name, dude. Not sure I believe all the religious stuff, but you're an okay guy."

Tommy smiled. "Tommy Richardson."
"Do you play football?" Jack responded.
"Yup." That was all Tommy needed to say.
"I saw you play Saturday. You're an amazing receiver."
"Tell you what, let's walk to the cafeteria; I'll buy coffee, let's chat."
With that, the three of them headed for the lunchroom.

As they reached the lunchroom, students gathered around his table. "Hey, guys, give a guy some room to just sit and have a cup of coffee. What's with all of this attention?" Inside he was smiling hugely. He knew that his fame was starting to get some attention.

Jayne, one of the students, smiled at Tommy. "Tommy Richardson, it's like this. You have been given a platform. Your prowess on the football field is what these kids are excited about. I want to see you at the next chapter meeting of the Intervarsity Christian Fellowship. I want to see you allow yourself to be used in a way that will touch the students. Fame is fleeting. You have a bad game, and you will be a goat. You allow yourself to be used by the Holy Spirit, and your "game" will be to be used by the Father of all mankind to see lives changed?"

Tommy got up from the table, walked across the room, and returned. His first reaction was a flash of anger. Thumbnail sitting on his shoulder said." Tommy settles down. Take a breath. She's right. You must realize that football is a game. You must realize those young kids will be looking up to you because of your prowess, and you must allow the Father of all mankind to use you to touch individuals around the country. There will come a time when you are playing your last game. It will be a big game, but it will be your last. Remember this. Through His Son by His Spirit, God the Father did not go to all the trouble to have Jill meet your mom and save your life for no reason. You will make a lot of money playing this kid's game. The question you must answer is this. Whose money is it? Are you going to save kids' lives or not? "Then Thumbnail left.

Tommy looked at Jayne and smiled. "I guess young lady, your right. It's time for me to get my head out of the clouds and be used for the Father's purpose and not mine."

Jayne looked at Tommy and said. "Tommy, there is an exec meeting on Monday afternoon in the Herman Johnson student center. I want you there. We are going to be planning the Christmas season. Speaking of seasons, yours is getting short. We work with First Church downtown. They have a hundred kids in their youth group. With the season you are having, you will be a huge hit with the kids."

Tommy smiled. "You know what? There may be some real opportunities to be reaching into the kids' lives. The Father plans these divine appointments with the greatest of care. Our role is to say what we are led to say today. He is responsible for the results. But we must be listening to the whole time for two things. What he is going to reveal about the young person we are speaking with, and what we should say to that young person."

Jayne smiled. "Tommy Richardson, I could just kiss you!" She said as she walked over to him and gave him a huge hug. In the back of her mind, she knew what she was thinking. "This guy is totally husband material. I could see myself spending the rest of my life with this guy. He would make a great dad to our kids. And oh, the kids we would have."

Tommy looked at Jayne. He did a double-take as he realized one underlying truth. "That young lady is drop-dead gorgeous." He thought.

- * -

The Father looked at Pete. "You know what, Pete. Putting my kids together is the best part of what I do. You see, I plan everyone. I know from the beginning which I have perfectly chosen for each other. With these two kids, the lightning is going to happen, but."

Pete knew not to ask questions. He understood the one thing that it took him years to learn. He would find it all out in God the Father's time and not a second before.

- * -

Jayne smiled at Tommy; thoughts started flooding her mind. Then she snapped back. "Tommy, let's put some things to work. Let me get in touch with the administration of the school. Do you think it would be possible to set up maybe 10 kids on the sideline for the final game of the year? It would be great P.R. for the team?"

Tommy smiled, "like the song says. Only believe; all things are possible if we only believe. But I do see some real pitfalls to this idea. But tell ya what, why don't you start to explore the possibilities. This could be great, or it could blow up in our face. God knows, and I don't have a clue."

Jayne took Tommy's hand and smiled at him. Her blue eyes twinkled in the lights. She smiled, and his heart melted. "Tommy, nothing worth doing comes easy."

Tommy smiled. "Jayne, it's like this. I was given life twice. Once by my mom, the second time by Jill McBrien. Like I said, I see a lot of pitfalls to this. I can see huge disappointment for all the young football players who don't get to be on the sidelines. But the negative may be outweighed by the positive. I think it is time to go to work. We must trust that the kids our Father in heaven want will be there. We must remember that the Father wants at that game will be there. He does not make mistakes."

Jayne smiled. Tommy Richardson, I think it's time I get to work. The last of the regular season is coming up fast. If I am going to make this happen, I must get to work. She then walked over to Tommy, put her hand on his shirt, and pulled him down to kiss him on the cheek. Tommy turned red.

The next few weeks were extremely busy for Jayne. She would be in contact with the league as well as the team. It was determined that the 10 boys would be dressed in the team's uniform. It was also determined that the players would be junior high football players. She had four weeks to pull it off. But pull it off, she did.

The big day arrived. The players were all in the dressing room. It was determined that the young players would be allowed to sit in on the coach's pregame talk to the players. The ten players all sat and listened intently as the complex plays were gone over with the offense and defense. The players would sit there wide-eyed as they were baffled by the complexity of the plays. The young players had expected that many of the same plays they were accustomed to would be used. They were totally overwhelmed by the plays they saw on the board.

There was excitement as Tommy's team left the locker room and the young boys with them. The young player would go through the warmups with the team. As they ran out onto the university's field, the crowd was going wild. The band was playing a tremendous fight song. The young boys were feeling part of something great. The two wide receivers in the group, Micky Johnson and Gabriel Smith were allowed to run some patterns with the College's own receivers.

John Jamison, Tommy's receiver coach, watched the young lads during warm-ups. He looked over at his assistant and said. "You know some amazing players are coming up. I can see how these kids could be a real asset in the future. Let's keep an eye on them through their high school years."

His assistant smiled. "Coach, your recruiting Tommy was a great move. His relationship with the young players is amazing. I can see these kids in a few years being just as important at the time they are here as Tommy is now."

Tommy would be the breakout player everyone knew he was during the game. He could make any quarterback he played with look exceptional, and the scouts knew it for many AFL teams. He was so quick that the opposing players would find themselves looking for their shoes after one of his quick "Jukes," He would catch 4 touchdown passes in this game.

5. THE DRAFT

On March 15th Tommy was in New York for the American Football League draft. He was sitting with his Mom Janet and his best friend, Jayne. The first player was about to be called. Dallas had the first pick. Tommy held his moms' hand on his left and Jayne's on the right. Dallas called his name. He dropped his head in his hands, stood up, raised his right hand, and gave out a big, "YES!!!"

He looked to his right and his left. Both loves of his life were smiling as broadly as he was. His mom was smiling as she leaned over to him. "You know what these means don't you?" She asked.

Tommy smiled and said. "Mom, let's talk about that later; I have to get up to the mic." He stood and walked up to the stage where the head guys for Dallas were standing. They took the jersey they had with them and held it up to him. His last name was on the back, and a big #1 was on the front. (Richardson) was at the top of the back of Jersey. His mom and Jayne had smiled so wide you could drive a semi through them. As he stood there, his mind returned to the day when he was just a lad.

The great Eli McBrien sat across from his mom and himself. He would get an autograph and a new life that day. He knew God the Father had "arranged" that day to save his life. As he stood there and looked out on the crowd as Dallas drafted him into pro football, he realized he was part of something bigger than himself. That the Father had a role for him to touch kids all over this country or even the world for that matter. He knew this adventure was just starting. He realized that the Father's platform had set up for him would be huge. He looked to heaven and prayed. "Father, use me in the role you have placed me in. Father, I pray that children and parents all this country will be pointed to you because of what you have done in me."

The M.C. of the draft asked Tommy if he had anything to say. Tommy realized that the Father had set this up as well. "Yes, sir, I do. I must thank my Father in heaven through his Son Jesus by his Holy Spirit for me being here today. My mother and I were having breakfast. I had just been diagnosed with terminal Leukemia. If I did not get a bone marrow transplant, I would die. I have a rare blood type. The great pitcher Eli McBrien and his bride Jill were sitting across from us. I was really a young lad. But the Father had huge plans for me. When I asked Eli for his autograph, I told him to autograph it for my mom because I would not be around long. Jill talked to my mom and was tested. She was a match. God arranged that appointment. I am here because God the Father, through His Son by His Spirit, has a role for me in his plan that has not been fulfilled. I need to complete my part of his plan.

The crowd went silent. The humility that Tommy Richardson was showing totally stunned the crowd. The entire crowd realized that Richardson was something special. Fred Johnson, the head of player personnel for Dallas, had a look of confusion on his face. He had no idea that Tommy Richardson had a history that would lend itself to so much positive public relations. He walked to the mic. "Folks, we are so pleased to have this young man coming to Dallas. Because of what the Lord has done in this young man, he will be a great football player for us, but we also hope he will continue the outreach to the young men coming up behind him. There are a great many young players at all levels that will be able to gain from this man's experiences both on and off the field." He turned shook Tommy's hand. Smiled at him and said. "Tommy, you ready to go to work?"

Tommy smiled back at him. "Let's get err done!" Then they turned, and both walked off the stage. Tommy walked onto the campus on Monday. Throughout his college career, he had not had the "hero worship" that he had experienced in high school. But, at this point in his career, he was okay with that. He realized that God was moving him into a position to be a role model for the young people coming up through the ranks. He also realized that he had to play at a level that would draw the young boys to him because of his athletic prowess. He thought back to his two-a-day experience in high school. His first experience with those was tough. Then he thought about his first two-a-day in college. Those were tougher.

Thumbnail jumped on his shoulder. "Boy, your about to experience what tough really is. But remember this. The toughness you will be going through to reach kids is nothing compared to what Jesus, the son of the Great I Am, went through so you could be here to sacrifice for all the kids he will use you to reach. Jesus, through the Holy Spirit, set this whole thing up so you could touch the kids he is bringing across your path. Never, I mean, never forget the restaurant that he used to bring you together with Jill McBrien to save your life to reach the kids.

The Father of all mankind will use people to reach other people. He will use screaming kids to reach other kids after those screaming kids get brought to me because of men like you."

Tommy looked around himself. "Who said that?" He knew the words he had just heard were true; he also knew that the work ahead of him would be hard. He just knew that the pain would be worth it. He also knew that the dollars he would earn playing a kid's game would turn many kids' lives around. He wasn't scared of the hard work; he was just looking forward to the pain of going through it. He understood that the pain would be for a short time, and because of the pain, he would be able to conquer those who would stop him from accomplishing what God the Father through Jesus wanted him to accomplish. He realized that generations of people not yet born would hear the word through those who would come to Christ because of him.

"Call Jill," Thumbnail whispered in his ear.
"What?" He asked.
"Call Jill." He heard again.

He shrugged and picked up his cell. He looked in his directory on the phone. No Jill or Eli McBrien. "Now what?" Went through his mind. He opened Google. "Google finds Eli McBrien, the former baseball player. His number popped up on his screen. Tommy could not believe his eyes. "This is unreal." He said as he dialed Eli's number.

"Eli here. Can I help you?"
"Eli, this is Tommy Richardson, remember me?"
"Tommy, of course. Jill is right here; would you like to speak with her?"

"Eli, that would be great." Was Tommy's exuberant response.

Jill came on the phone. "Jill, this is Tommy Richardson. How are you?"

Jill smiled. "Tommy, I am great. We have been following your college career and saw the draft last week. We are so excited for you. Our son Herman watched the draft with us. He is 14 and going to be playing for Carlton this year. He is beside himself, watching you. He is a great young quarterback; he says he would love to throw to you. He does realize that will probably not happen, but it is his dream."

Tommy smiled. "Let's see what happens. Considering he is a freshman, he has 4 years of high school, 4 years of college, then he must get drafted. It's a stretch, but we do serve the awesome God, do we not?"

Jill smiled. "Tommy, that we do. We will see just how hard Hermie is willing to work. We both know that our Father in heaven gives the gifts. It's how hard are we willing to work with those gifts that will make us great in the kingdom, or another just so believer. The choice is ours."

Tommy sat with the phone to his ear, nodding. "Jill, I would not even be here if the Father had not worked out that meeting years back. I really don't feel I have that much choice. The Father used you to give me a chance. I have used it the best I could. I just feel like God the Father wants to use your son Herman in some really special way as well. I just sense the Father wants to use the lad. If he is willing to work hard, I really feel like The Father will give him victories that will astound people. The question is this. How hard is he willing to work? Just not sure what that will look like."

Jill smiled. "Tommy, I am really impressed with what you are doing with your life. I know this; our Father will use you to touch kids. Don't worry about Hermie; the Father has his role in His plan all set. Let's just pray that what the Father is going to do with you guys will bring glory to him and lots of kids into his kingdom."

Tommy smiled broadly. "Give my best to both Herm and Eli. You have got a couple of great men there. Just know this. God will use Herman if he is willing to work hard."

The next morning Jayne called Tommy. Tommy answered his cell. "Good morning, sweet one. How is your day starting out?" He asked.

Tommy could hear Jayne sobbing on the other end. "Tommy, I am really happy and proud of you. You have accomplished the dream of every football player. But you know I have had a dream as well. My dream is to take me to Alaska to work with the fish and game up there to ensure the Salmon population stays strong. I wanted to do it in person, but I am afraid this will be goodbye. I think the Father had us together for a season, to reach kids, that's over. I wish you well." With that, she hung up.

Tommy was hit with a 2x4 in the head with that one. He did not quite know how to handle it. What he did know was that the Father would use them both over their lives; if he brought them back together, that would be great; if not, that would be his will, and Tommy would have to live with that.

6. TRAINING CAMP

After traveling to Dallas, Tommy found his way to the training center. He realized that his instant stardom from high school and college was gone as he walked in. Coach Norland walked up to him and smiled. "Tommy, get ready for some hard work, no let me put that a different way. This is going to be brutal for you. You are the best of the best, but keep this in mind, you will be competing against the best of the best. Every cornerback, every linebacker you compete against, will be as good as you are. We are going to work you hard. So, get ready."

"Coach, you guys are paying me a lot of money. I need to earn it. Let's make some things happen and see if we can win a championship." Tommy answered. With that, Tommy turned and walked into the dorm. He walked to the counter where the room assignments were being made.

The guy behind the counter looked at Tommy. "Your rooming with Jamaal Smith." Handed Tommy his key. Tommy went to the dorm room, walked in, and saw a man's giant. "You must be Jamaal?" Tommy asked.

Thumbnail jumped on Tommy's shoulder. "Tommy, you are about to educate Jamaal on what it means to be a child of the King."

Jamaal looked at Tommy. "You must be that new hotshot receiver, eh? We rarely see someone of your kind being fast enough to play at this level." He said.

Tommy had played at all levels of the sport that he loved. "I can see there is some underlying prejudice going on here. I have a question for you. Who's imagine are we created in?" Tommy asked.

"What do you mean?" Jamaal answered.

"Listen, Jamaal. Our Father in heaven likes variety. If we go back to Genesis, one of the first things it says is this. Let us create man in our image. We are all children of the king. So, let's get beyond that color thing, shall we?" Tommy said.

Jamaal smiled. "Man, I never thought of it in that light. I am going to make sure Tate can get the ball to you. I got your back. You're a great friend. I can see that now."

_ * _

The Father looked at Pete and winked. "Pete, Tommy was right. I created all colors of people. But the fakeness comes in is what the enemy of man's souls does with all the fake 'religions.' Just watch the bond I build between these two ballplayers. They will both have long careers with Dallas. The next thing to watch is what I do with the last year Tommy plays in Dallas before I take him back to Minnesota. Things are going to be amazing for a year. Just watch. Tommy thought he was sore after his first college practice. That is going to seem like a cakewalk to what he is about to go through." The Father said with a chuckle.

_ * _

The next morning, 530 A.M sharp, Tommy heard a drill, Sargent. "Alright, momma's boys, out of those bunks. You are being paid some big money; you still must make the team. You are in the real world now. Let's get to work." Tommy crawled out of his bunk, threw on his workout gear, and hit the field. They would spend the next 4 hours in a grueling workout with shoulder pads, cleats, and shorts. Never in his wildest dream did he know that a workout could be this demanding. He found himself practically crawling back to the dorm. Johnson, the trainer, walked up to him.

"Richardson, when the game is on the line, you must have something left in the tank. All these workouts are making the "tank" that much bigger. When It's 4th down and 10 yards to go, 5 seconds left in the game, and you must run one pattern to win or lose, and it's 65 yards to the end zone, you gotta be able to burn a defender.

Remember, we are paid to win. We are paid to show what it really means to leave it all on the field. You won't be playing football for the rest of your life. You may have 10, maybe 15 years in you. The better shape you can get yourself into now, the easier it will be to maintain it until the end of your career.

Tommy walked to his room. Dropped onto the bed and just laid there for two hours. He woke at 2:30 and realized he had to get to a team meeting in 5 minutes. When he got to the meeting, the applause rang out. He looked to his left and right; all the vets were smiling, some laughing. "Richardson, you're the last one here. You get to come up to the front and do a chicken dance for all of us. Johnson said, laughing.

Tommy looked at Johnson shaking his head. "You can't be serious?" He asked.

"Not only am I serious, but we also want to hear clucking as you do the dance," Johnson said, laughing.

Tommy would spend the next 10 minutes doing the chicken dance in front of 80 other football players. After everyone got done with their laughs, the whole team settled down to getting ready for the season. Tommy had thoughts about stopping such activity and brutality to the rookies coming in after the next year. Then he thought of the hundreds of people who survived it. He realized that such activity broke the tension and built a comradeship among the players to carry them through the season. He laid on his bunk. Started chuckling quietly, then louder.

Jones, his roommate, asked him what he was laughing about. "The chicken dance." That was all that Tommy had to say.

"The Chicken dance?" Jones responded.

"I was thinking about what all that laughter does for the team. Granted, it is a bit dehumanizing for the rookies having to do it. But in the long run, the effects of it are positive. Just good fun." Tommy said, still laughing.

As Tommy walked out after practice, a young man named Jon Goldsmith walked up to him. "Mr. Richardson, could I get your autograph?" The young lad asked.

Tommy gave Jon a huge smile. Walked over to him and said. "What's your name, young man?"

"I am Jon Goldsmith." The lad responded.

Tommy smiled at him. "Jon, did you ever hear about how my getting an Autograph from the great Eli McBrien saved my life?"

"No sir, I have not." The boy answered.

"Well, I was about your age; I had leukemia and did not have long to live. After my Doctor's appointment, my mom took me out to this fancy restaurant for breakfast. Eli and his wife, Jill, were sitting across from us. I got a piece of a notebook from my mom. When I told Eli and Jill what was wrong with me when I asked him to sign it for my mom, Jill got up and walked over to talk to my mom. We were to find out that Jill has the same blood type that I do. She donated bone marrow; I am still alive and playing pro football. I think God our Father has something for me to do. Other than football, I am not really sure what that is now."

Jon looked at him with a serious look on his face. "What's God?" He asked.

That question hit Tommy like a ton of bricks. He lifted his face toward heaven and had a prayer he wished he could scream, but he prayed it in silence. "Father, help!" Tommy screamed that prayer in silence. He knew there was an answer; he just did not know how to answer it. Tommy looked at the young boy and asked him what his age was.

"I am 7. The young Jon answered.

"Jon, it's like this. Do you see that car across the street?" Tommy asked.

"Yes, what about it?" Tommy answered.

"For that car to be there, someone had to build it, right?" Tommy said.

"I suppose," Jon answered.

"Jon, your body is much more complex than any machine that is known to man. A car is not designed to fix itself. The human body is. Yet because of how complex we are, we could not have just happened; each one of us was built." "God, however, wanted someone to love. He wanted someone who could love him back. God the Father created to love. The bible tells us he is love. But for there to be love, there must be a choice not to love. Hence, God the Father created us in his image. He chooses to love us. We have a choice to love him back. Do you understand this?" Tommy said.

Jon smiled at Tommy. "I think so. But remember, I am only 7. But I am starting to get it a little bit."

Tommy reached inside his jacket. "Jon, here are three tickets to Sunday's game. One for your mom, dad, and yourself. Do you have any brothers or sisters?"

"Nope, and my dad was a soldier; he was killed overseas. It's just mom and me." Jon said with a tear running down his cheek.'

Just then, Tommy felt a tap on his shoulder. "I hope my son is not causing any trouble?" The attractive woman behind him said. "I am Jon's mom."

"Hi! I am Tommy Richardson." "And your name is?" Tommy answered.

Kate smiled at Tommy. "I am Kate Goldsmith, Jon's mom. A pleasure to meet you. What do you do, Mr. Richardson?" Kate asked.

"I am the new receiver for Dallas. I play football." Tommy answered.

At that second, Jon piped up. "Mom, I love football; Mr. Tommy just gave me these tickets for the game Sunday. Can we go, please?" Jon asked.

_ * _

The Father smiled. "Pete, can you see what I am doing here? This little boy needs a daddy desperately. I am going to use Tommy to bring Kate closer to me. She still blames me for the death of her husband. I am going to show her what love looks like here." The Father stated with his full majesty.

Pete smiled. "You are not going to give me even a small clue as to what you're going to do, are you?"

The Father chuckled and said. "Stay tuned, Pete, just stay tuned."

_ * _

"Did I hear you talking to my Son about God?" Kate asked with a somewhat intense tone in her voice.

"Kate, I sure did," Tommy answered.

"Why?" Kate asked.

"Kate, it's like this. I told him about how Eli's McBriens wife saved my life. I mentioned how God the Father set up the whole thing so I could live. He asked me, 'what's god?' I explained God to him."

Tommy could see the anger in her eyes. "There is no God. A loving God would not have allowed my husband to be killed overseas."

Tommy reached out and put his hand on her shoulder. "Listen, I don't have all the answers, but this I know. Man is sinful. Men screw up. And men are killed because of sin. May I ask what happened?"

"I have been told they were just out on patrol. The Muslims sent a little boy out with a bomb attached to his waist. My husband picked him up, and the little boy blew up in my husband's arms, killing both of them."

Tommy could see the tears starting to flow like a river down her cheek. She looked at Tommy and threw her arms around his neck. She held him tightly for a couple of minutes. Then she stepped back, her face red from crying and embarrassment.

"Mr. Richardson, I am so sorry. Here you have been very nice to my son and almost exploded on you. I am so sorry. What can I do to make it up to you?" She asked.

Tommy looked to heaven for just a second. "Dinner at your house. A good homecooked meal. I have not had one in an awfully long time." Tommy answered.

Now Katie was getting really embarrassed. "Do you want just you and me, or is Jon welcome as well?" She had not expected that response. But she knew she had to follow through.

Tommy turned to Jon, Picked the lad up, and put him on his shoulders. "Of course! he is welcome. I would like nothing better than to have this young lad sitting on my shoulder to have dinner with us."

Tommy looked at Kate. "You do realize I will need your address?"
"We have not set a date yet, Mr. Richardson." She said.
"When would be convenient for you?" Tommy asked.
"Let's do Sunday night after your game." She responded.

"I'll be there," Tommy responded. But before I come to your house, you have to come to mine. Here are some box seat tickets to Sunday's game. I hope you enjoy it?"

Jon's eyes got big a saucer. He looked at his mom, and his smile was so big you could almost drive a truck through it.

"Should I be there at 6"? Tommy asked.
"Perfect." Was Kate's answer.

7. DINNER WITH KATE AND JON

As Kate and Jon walked to the ticket gate, they had no idea how to get to their seats. They were about to find out that their seats were not just seats; they would be in a penthouse overlooking the stadium. Jon was beside himself as they walked in and saw all the great food laid out for them. Kate thought to herself. "How are we going to eat tonight after all this good food here?"

All through the game, Jon's excitement grew and grew. Every catch that Tommy made, made Jon that much more excited. The score of this game would be totally lopsided as Dallas would exterminate Cleveland from 36 to 20.

After the game, Tommy walked up and knocked on the door. "I thought you just might like a desert. I realized that the stadium fed you quite well. How about we make some coke floats and just enjoy the evening together?"

Kate smiled at Tommy and put her fingers up to her lips. She pointed to the couch where Jon was out cold from excitement. "Let's be quiet; I think he may be down for the count. I have never seen him as excited as he watched you score three touchdowns." At that second, Jon started to move. His eyes opened slowly, then he jumped off the couch.

"Mr. Richardson, you were great today. Can you show me how to catch a football like that?" Jon asked.

Tommy smiled at Jon. "Young man, I think that can be arranged. But not tonight, okay. It's been a terribly busy day for me. What do you say we relax today? I will arrange for your mom to bring you out to the field to see how the pros do it." He said.

_ * _

The Father smiled. "Pete, I started planning this the second her husband came to be with me. I have already discussed with him who I would have raised his son." The Father then pointed to Jim, watching Tommy connect with Jon. Both tears and smiles were coming from Jim. He would love to be there raising his son. Yet he trusted The Father to put a man in his place who would raise him to fear and trust the Lord with his very being."

_*_

After dinner, Tommy got on the phone with his coach, "Coach Norland, I have this young lad who would love to be able to catch a ball as well as I do. Do you think we could bring him out to practice so he could see how the pros do it?"

"What is the age of our new recruit?" to coach asked.

Tommy smiled to himself. "Seven."

Coach Norland smiled. "Tell him I am always looking for the future. We will give him a good look, and he can give us one as well." The coach said with a chuckle. "You can also tell him if I like what I see; we may just dress him for the game next Sunday."

"Coach, I think I would like to bring him into practice on Tuesday of next week. That will give us time to get everything cleared with his teacher at school." Tommy thought to himself, "This should be fun!"

Coach Norland smiled and said. "I think I will have Jackson throw him a couple of passes. If he catches them ok, I will have him go out for a pass at the stadium before the game. That will give him a thrill of a lifetime, and the crowd will love it.

Kate brought Jon to practice. The team had a practice uniform ready for Jon. Jon was so excited he was jumping all over the place

The next few days, after practice, Tommy would be spending his time throwing to Jon. Jon was a natural. Tommy started throwing light passes, which got harder and harder. Jon was catching everything. The day came when he would be in front of Coach Lundberg to catch passes from Curt Jackson.

Jackson threw a light one, which Jon snagged without a problem. Jackson got a surprised look on his face. He threw a little harder; again, Jon grabbed it and tucked it under his arm while in full stride. Time after time, Jon would catch the passes. But Sunday was coming. The question came to the coach's mind. 'Would Jon be able to catch the ball in front of thousands of fans?'

Suddenly it was Sunday morning. Jon had said nothing to the kids in his class. But the paper got word of what would happen that day at the stadium. His whole class would be tuned in to the game that Sunday.

Jon joined the team in the dressing room and put on his "game" uniform. He looked around himself and saw monsters of men walking around him. They all were being genuinely nice to him. Jon was allowed to sit in on the coach's pre-game speech. Jon really felt like part of the team. Finally, it was time to go.

As the team stood at the stadium's opening, waiting to be allowed onto the field, Jon was at the front of the line. His classmates were glued to the televisions with their dads watching the pregame. They all saw Jackson throw the first pass to Jon. Jon made a perfect catch. His smile lit up the stadium.

The announcer Tom Sullivan said, "Folks, what you are seeing is the next great receiver for Dallas. This kid is only 7 years old and can snatch out of the air any pass Jackson throws his way. I went to the "tryout," they gave this kid. I saw him catch some passes he should not have. He is amazing with what he can do."

Tommy would catch two touchdown passes as Dallas would take the victory from Denver. The game was over; Dallas won 27 to 21. There was a lot of hooting and hollering in the locker room. The coach walked in, smiling; he said, "well, gents, that's one more under our belt. Let's go home and enjoy the rest of the day; see you back here on Tuesday.

Monday, Jon walked into his classroom. His mom had washed his jersey Sunday night, so he could wear it again on Monday. The class went nuts. All the other kids were excited that Jon had done such a great job catching the football. Suddenly, he went from being a dude to a hero.

Mrs. Johnson had a light go on inside of her head. But how was she going to pull it off? She looked to heaven and said a little prayer. "Father in heaven, I know there is a teaching moment here, but how do I handle this.

- * -

"Pete, I know what has to be done here. You see, when I put the gift of teaching in people at conception, I do it for the reason of moments just like this. Mrs. Johnson has served me all her life. She has taught thousands of my children live's lessons. This is of huge importance. Watch what I do here." The Father said.

- * -

Mrs. Johnson smiled. She pulled Jon aside. "Jon, do you think you could get Mr. Richardson to come to class to visit us.?"

Jon shrugged. "I don't know; I can ask him and see what he says."

"Jon, here is my cell phone number; if he is willing, I have a special reason for asking him. Please have him call me." She said.

That night Tommy came to Kate and Jon's home. Jon came running out of his room and handed Tommy the note from his teacher. Jon had not read it as Mrs. Johnson sealed it in an envelope so only Tommy would see it. Tommy opened the envelope. "Mr. Richardson, the kids in my classroom have a little problem. Before Jon had his day with your football team, he was not one of the 'in crowd' in his classroom. Now he is. The problem is not that he is popular now; he was not before. He is the same kid. He became a hero because he could catch a football, and he knew you. He is the same kid. Would you be willing to come to my classroom and speak about this problem with his classmates? You see, I think they should all be treating each other like the hero's they are. God has given us all gifts. Those gifts are to be used to see lives touched. We are all heroes to someone."

Tommy smiled as he picked up his cell phone. "Hello, Mrs. Johnson. Tommy Richardson here. Let's set up for me to be there next Monday." Tommy hung up the phone, looked at Jon, and said. "Partner, it's set up." He did not tell him when as agreed with Mrs. Johnson to give away the plan.

Katie called Jon over to sit on her lap. "Sweetheart, you know you can't say a word about Tommy coming to your classroom, don't you."

Jon smiled at her. "Mommy, I know this. God has Tommy coming to my classroom for a reason. The surprise is part of it. It will be hard, but I will not say a word." With that, Katie gave Jon a huge hug.

The next few days in school were very tough for Jon. He wanted to share what he knew would happen but knew he could not. He did not know the time or the hour when Tommy would walk into the room.

Then it hit him. He had heard in church that Jesus was going to return. He just did not know the day or the time. He just had to believe that Jesus was going to return.

It was Thursday afternoon. Jon was busy doing his math. He did not hear the door open and close. Suddenly he felt a hand on his shoulder. He looked up, and Tommy was standing over him. He jumped up from his seat into Tommy's arms. He then looked over and saw his mom standing at the front of the class.

Tommy would spend the next hour sharing how football is like life in general with Jon's class. The more a team works together, the more success they have. But Tommy had one other thing in mind. He felt that there was no better place to do what he really wanted to do. He called Katie to the front of the class. He got down on one knee and asked her to be his bride forever. She said YES!

Jon's face lit up. He got up out of his seat and started jumping all over the place. His joy could not be hidden. Then it hit him. His mom would marry someone that the Father through the Son brought into their lives. He had to ask this question in silence. "What would his dad in heaven think of this?"

_ * _

The Father looked at Jon's dad sitting before him. "What do you think of Katy and Tommy being made one in me?" The Father asked Jon's dad.

All he could do was smile. "Father, you are in charge of everything. I know you have put Katie and Tommy together. You also know that the son you gave me to carry on my name needs a solid Father on the earth to lead my son to you and raise him up to be used by you to bring other people to yourself. I praise you for taking care of the son you gave me. I have only one request. Could you send me back tonight to stand beside my son's bed? I would like to tell him that Tommy is a man after your heart and to trust him as he would trust me?"

The Father thought for a moment. Then he spoke. "Normally, I don't let people go back. But I am going to make an exception to this. Tonight, you will find yourself in Jon's room. Touch him, and he will feel your touch. He will wake and sit up in bed. Tell him who you are and that I have chosen Tommy as his stepfather and what you really think of the whole idea. Enjoy those few moments you will have with your son. "

- * -

That night Jon's dad found himself beside Jon's bed. He looked at his sleeping son and realized that his yearning to see the greatness in his son was huge. He also realized that the man to bring that out was Tommy. He longed to be the one who could lead his son to accomplish all that the Father through Jesus for him to accomplish. He also realized that his form was physical and a spirit. He did not understand it, but he knew that His Father in heaven did. He sat on the bed. He could feel it under himself. He spoke.

"Jonathon." Jon stirred. "Jonathon, my son." Jonathon opened his eyes. He looked and saw his dad.
"Dad, is that you?" He asked.

"It's me, Jon. I only have a few moments to spend with you. First, I need to tell you this. God the Father loves you so very much. Second, I love you more than you will be able to understand on this earth. Third, because the Father loves you so much, he had Tommy come into your life. As much as I would love to, I can't be in your life. But we are given time right now to talk and share Father, son time with each other. This I need to tell you. I met your mother in college; I walked into the Intervarsity Christian Fellowship office. There was this beautiful blonde, Your mother. I was smitten; we would spend the next two and a half hours talking about Jesus Christ sitting on lounge chairs in the student center. I loved your mom more than life itself. I never got to spend time with you while I was on the earth. That is why I am so grateful to the Father for giving me this brief time to spend with you."

Jon reached up to his dad, put his hand on his dad's arm. "Dad, can I hug you?" Jon asked with a tear in his eye.

His dad reached down, took his son into his arms, and held him as only a Father could.

The light of God the Father glowed from Jon's dad. They would spend the next two hours talking and touching each other. Jon was able to sit on his dad's lap for a while and feel the closeness only a

Father and Son could feel.

Katie walked by the door. She could see the light shining from under the door. She touched the handle of the door and opened it. All she could see was a bright light and Jon sitting inside it. Thumbnail sitting on her shoulder said. "It's his dad; he can see him; the Father has granted him this time to let him know that the Father has granted something he rarely does. A visit. Shut the door and walk away." Katie did as she was told.

The next morning, Jon came bouncing down the stairs. "Mom, you will never believe what happened last night." He said excitedly.

Katie knew exactly what happened and responded. "And what my son might that be?"

Jon smiled. "Dad came and sat on my bed; we talked for a long time. He thinks you marrying Tommy is a great idea."

Katie smiled, knowing what her son was telling her was the truth. "I was wondering what that bright light inside your room was. I am so happy you got to spend some time with your dad and get to know him just a bit. I feel really good about what the Father will do with you. Now you must eat some of this breakfast, son, and get ready for school. Oh! It's probably better if you don't mention this to any of your friends in school, though."

Jon smiled and said. "Mom, they would never believe it. I would be laughed out of my class. But it did happen; I will remember it the rest of my life."

8. THE START OF SOMETHING BIG

Dallas was headed for the Playoffs. Because of it, Tommy knew he had not had the time to invest in Jon the way he really wanted to. He also knew that would end shortly. The team was focused, and he knew that a good performance would also mean big bonuses for the team and their families. Tommy was coming to understand one thing about pro sports. The more the team wins, the more money everyone makes. After practice, he drove to Katie's house. He walked inside and plopped down on the couch. Tommy came running into the room and saw Tommy half asleep on the couch. He walked over and sat down. He looked at Tommy and asked a question that would have Tommy thinking for a long time.

"Tommy, what difference does a football or any sport have on the big picture. What I mean is this. How can a game change someone's life for the better or worse?"

"Tommy, I hear you talking about Jesus a lot." In the back of his mind, he had the visit that he had had with his dad in his bedroom in mind. "What difference can He make in a person's life?"

As Tommy smiled, A bolt of lightning hit him. "Jon, Jesus touches lives. He uses us and the gifts we have been given to do the touching. My ability to catch a football gives me a platform to share Christ with people of all ages. That's the importance of football."

Jon, at that second, had a huge smile on his face. "When did you know you would be a great football player? He asked.

Tommy got a real serious look on his face. "It's like this, son. It's not when I knew I was a good player; the hard work I put into it took me from an average player to where I am now. No one could catch me as I played with my buddies on the school ground. When I played football in middle school, I realized I did not drop many balls. As I worked in High School, I realized the harder I worked, the better I became. I have a question for you. How hard are you willing to work to become the player that God the Father through His Son Jesus by His Holy Spirit created you to be? How hard are you really willing to work to achieve it?"

Jon's face contorted a bit. "You mean greatness just doesn't happen; one has to work to become great?" Jon asked.

"Jon, it's like this. Before we are conceived, the Father, through the Son by the Spirit, had instilled in us everything we need to succeed. However, that success can only happen when we work our tails off to be the best we can be with the gifts we have been given. A gift does no one any good whatsoever if it is not used. Our Father gives gifts to be used. Remember Jesus when he told the parable of the gifts. One was given 5, one 3, and one 1. The guy with one did nothing with it. Jesus told us that he was cast into outer darkness. The other two doubled their gifts and were rewarded.

"Tommy, who do you play Sunday?" Jon asked.

"Washington." Was Tommy's answer. "If you and your mom want to come, I will get you in the skybox," Tommy answered.

All Jon had to do was look at his mom. She smiled and asked Tommy one question. "What time should we be at the stadium?"

"The game starts at noon; I would suggest you arrive at about 11:00. You will have refreshments in your skybox, and your view of the game will be great.

Jon's excitement was almost uncontrollable. He was jumping up and down. His smiles were so broad and bright that his excitement was lighting up the room.

Tommy could not help but smile. "Jon, if the Lord sees fit for me to catch a touchdown pass today, I am going to point to heaven; when I do that, I want you to just listen. I think you will hear what I say then.

That Sunday, as Tommy ran onto the field, he could feel an excitement he had not felt in a long time. He looked at Josh Adams across the field. Josh would be covering him that day. He could feel the Holy Spirit envelop him. The warmth he was feeling was like none that he had felt before. He knew that this day was going to be special.

The game would prove to be tough. They had 80 yards to go for the win. But when Tommy's quarterback walked into the huddle with them trailing by 3 with 30 seconds left and called 95 sprints, Tommy knew this was his shot. He knew he had to smoke Josh and get the catch for the touchdown. Thompson, his quarterback, called out the signals. The ball snapped. Tommy turned on the afterburners, and Adams tried to catch Tommy from behind. As Tommy crossed the goal line, he smiled and pointed to heaven. "Jim, this one's for you!"

Jon sitting in the Penthouse with the other players' families, heard Tommy tell his dad those 4 words. "Jim, this one's for you!" Jon started to cry.

Katie looked at Jon crying. "What's going on?" She asked him.

"Mom, I heard Tommy tell Dad that that touchdown was for him. He kept his promise."

All Kate could do was smile. She, too, had a tear in her eye. She knew that God the Father, through his Son Jesus by His Holy Spirit, had put this whole thing together just for her son. She realized how important Tommy would be for Jonathon as he grew into a man.

The next few years would prove to be valuable for Jon. He grew quickly and would become a great lineman even at the middle school level. He would gain a love for football that anyone could not match.

At the same time, Tommy's mind kept going back to the young quarterback. Herman McBrien. He could not help but think that as this young man made his way through school, his career would be going on towards its end. He looked to heaven and prayed. "Father, give me just one year with Herman. If you have designed him for the pros, give me just one year with him."

- * -

The Father looked at Peter. "Pete, I am going to give him one year with Herman. Just watch what I have in mind for those two. Not only am I going to use them for my purpose, but they are going to have a great deal of fun doing it."

Peter looked at the Father. "Father, you're not even going to give me a hint, are you?"

The Father chuckled. "Nope." That was all he had to say.

- * -

Katie could hardly contain the tears. She knew that the Father had just done something amazing for Jon. Jon was a young man that the Father had big plans for. She knew the Father had him conceived even knowing that his father would not spend any time raising him. But she also knew, because of what she witnessed in his room, that the Father had set up for her to meet Tommy, and Tommy would become the Dad in his life.

The playoffs were coming. Tommy knew that more time would be away from his family during that stretch. But he knew that the money he was making during the season would make it possible during the offseason to spend the quality time he needed to help shape Jon into the man he was created to be. Jon was about to learn that no matter what, when the prize was to be won, one had to keep their eyes on the prize. One could not look to the right or the left but focused on the prize. In Tommy's case, the prize would be another Superbowl victory; however, the prize in life had to be Christ. Tommy would catch two touchdown passes in the Superbowl against L.A., and the season would be over.

After the game and a huge celebration, there would be a letdown. He looked around himself as he walked into his home. He looked at his beautiful bride and asked one question. "So What?"

Katie looked at Tommy. "So what?" She asked.

"Ya, So what. I know part of this is to set up a platform to speak into people's lives, but other than that, what difference in the whole scheme of things does it make? We won the Superbowl, so what. Just does not make any sense at all to me. But I must remember this. I am given the gifts to be able to play this sport. I enjoy playing it. It's just these emotional letdowns; whether we win or lose the big game, there is always a letdown. I'll be back. Next season, I sense that there is something big about to happen. Let's just see how everything plays out.

Tommy being in his 6th year was watching the progression of Herman McBrien. Herman was entering his Junior year of Collegiate football and was breaking every passing record. He was wishing it would be April of this year but knew it would be a couple more years until Herman's shot at the pros; he would find that Dallas had something special in mind in their draft this year. Herman was unaware of who it was, but he knew and understood that they had in mind their dominance over everyone else in the league.

Finally, the day arrived. Tommy had his tv on watching the draft. Dallas's first player would pick Gregg Shoemaker from Eau Clair state in the first round. His speed was phenomenal. His hands were considered the best in the league. Tommy looked at Dallas's tenure so far and realized they were looking to the future. But he also realized that Dallas' passing attack would be unstoppable for the next couple of years. He looked at Katie and said. "This should be fun."

9. THE FUN STARTS

Gregg Shoemaker!

Spring and summer came and went. It was time for training camp to start for Tommy. He saw a new face beside him in the locker room as he walked in. "And who might you be?" Tommy asked.

"I am your new tailback. My name is Gregg Shoemaker." Was Greggs response.

"Where are you from?" Tommy asked.

"I was raised on a little farm near a small hamlet in Wisconsin. The town's name was Marilyn. "

"And your college ball?" Tommy asked

"Eau Clair state." That was his answer.

"And you think you can make this pro team? Granted, you probably looked fairly good on the field, but we will see what you can do here." Tommy responded, fully expecting him to be gone after the first week of training camp.

As they walked out for the opening wind sprints, Gregg smiled to himself. "I know this guy is fast. I have seen him outrun every cornerback in the country. Let's see what he can do with me in the sprints," He thought; Dallas had a new coach. Coach Wolf, the new back coach, called them to the line. Gregg lined up beside Tommy and smiled. Looked over at Tommy. "Good luck." He said, smiling ear to ear. The whistle blew. Greg blew Tommy away. As they finished the

40-yard sprint, the look on Tommy's face was one of total amazement.

"I want a rematch!" Tommy said to Gregg.

"You got it, bro. Let's go."

[...], but Gregg still won. Tommy was beside [...] the 40, but this kid was beating him every [...] ought (Sunday, man, you put this kid and [...] will have a real winning combination. This [...] p dragged on and on. Finally, the regular [...]

[...] ohnson came in from the sidelines with the [...] d coach. Jack Osborn, the head coach, had [...] d to the test early. Tim came to the huddle [...] clear bomb drop on set. Both Tommy and [...] g called. They would both fly and let the [...] Hut!" was called, and they both headed for [...] The defense could not even come close to [...] the ball towards Shoemaker, who caught it [...] his first touchdown as a pro on the game's [...]

[...] mmy and Gregg together would prove to be a magical blowout. Dallas would win 57 to 7. It would also prove to be a bonding experience that would bind the two men together as brothers for the rest of their careers, even after Gregg would be traded 4 years later. The ministry that would be started with this brotherhood would continue for years to come.

Monday morning, Tommy invited Gregg over for breakfast. When he knocked on the door, Katie greeted him with a smile. "You must be the great Gregg Shoemaker that totally frustrated Tommy. He tells me that he could not beat you in the 40, but the two of you cleaned house on all of the defenders in the last game."

Being the humble guy he was, Gregg got red in the face. "Yup, that would be me. But I have a great deal to learn yet. I am just going to follow Tommy's lead on things. Things will be great; I have a great deal to learn. But what I really want to tap into is his relationship to Christ. Once a person has that down, Jesus can magnify those gifts to bring more glory to himself."

The next week's preparation for the Minnesota game would be nothing short of brutal. They worked and worked to get every pass on the spot. They knew that they had to have their game perfect to beat the Minnesota Norseman. No dropped passes. They went over and over the pass routes. They knew the game would be brutal. But they also understood the parable of the talents. They had purposed within themselves that the mission was to maximize their talents to garner the admiration of the young football fans. By doing so, they would be able to speak into their lives.

The game was magical. Dallas would put Minnesota on the ropes in the first quarter. Three touchdowns on the first three possessions. The game would end with a record-breaking score. 55 to 20 Dallas was the victor.

As they walked into the dressing room, Tommy and Gregg could not help but wonder. "What's the point?" They had just had a huge victory, but what is the point. Why play a game that has no effect whatsoever on anyone's life at all? They looked at each other. They knew what the other was thinking. Then it hit them. The game itself does not have to have any long-term impact on anyone. The impact from anything we do serving the risen Christ has to be speaking into the lives that can be changed. The impact goes back to the parable of the talents. Hard work produces results. Those results can be victories on a football field that translate into speaking to young people about the value of pouring oneself into the Father's talents through the Son by the Spirit gives them.

As Gregg walked out of the locker room, an attractive young female reporter was waiting for him. "Mr. Shoemaker, you played a great game. You have a great many young people wanting to hear from you. Do you have anything to say to them?"

"I do; it's like this; our Father in heaven has given each of us gifts. Yours can take a story and bring it across to grasp what is going on in the world. We each have a role. A carpenter builds or repairs houses. A mechanic fixes cars. I catch footballs. We must use that ability given to us to touch lives." Gregg said.

Jean, the reporter, then got a sly grin on her face. She asked. "Mr. Shoemaker, every gift you spoke of except one contributes something to society. Would you tell me how football contributes to society?"

Gregg thought for just a moment. "My dear: it's like this. We are entertainment. It's the classic good versus evil scenario. A town's team is a rallying cry against the other towns' team. For a few hours, the folks of the community, whether it be Pro, or High School, or even elementary school, can come together for a brief time and put forth a united front." He said.

Jean then asked a question that opened doors. "Mr. Shoemaker. What difference has the sport made in your life?"

Gregg smiled. "It's opened lots of doors. For instance, if I were not having a great season on the football field, an attractive young reporter like yourself would have little interest in just another guy on the street, would you?"

Jean, a bit red-faced, smiled as she said. "I suppose your right, but what do you do with those open doors?"

At this point, Gregg had many thoughts go through his mind. He knew he could not talk about the ministry as he did not want people shying away from him because they thought he would get "religious" on them. He looked at Jean and said. "Off the record?"

Jean answered. "Okay."

"Let's have dinner." He responded.

"Can I bring my husband?" That was her answer.

"Of course. I did not see a ring, so I..."

Jean smile. "Gotcha. I would love to have dinner with you. But now tell me about your work with kids." She said.

"It's like this. Have you ever read Jesus' parable of the talents?" He asked.

Jean got a quizzical look on her face. "Yes, I have read that?" She answered.

"Jean, like I said just a few moments ago. We are all given gifts. I try to get the Father's children through His Son Jesus brings across my path to think in those terms. When a young person recognizes their talents at a young age, it gives them the ability to really develop those talents into all that our Father in heaven would have them be."

Jean smiled." Gregg, I am beginning to see the value of sport."

Gregg answered. "Let's continue this over dinner tonight?"

"Sound good. Where?"

"The Place on 21st."

"See you there," Jean answered.

Gregg walked out and started to walk for his car. He looked to heaven and prayed. "Father, what are you doing here? She is an amazing woman; could it be that you are starting something here that will last an eternity? Could this be the start of something amazing?

_ * _

In Heaven, the angels of God the Father were getting excited as they did every time the Father, through His Son by His Spirit, touched people and began an eternal relationship between a man and woman. The Father looked at St Peter and smiled. "Pete, when I 'arrange' these types of relationships, my excitement level explodes. This couple will be together forever. Oh, they will be apart for a few years when one of them leaves the earth first to join me here, but after a time, I will bring them back together for eternity. This is so much fun. I love it when the whole death do us part happens; it actually opens things up; it throws open the door of eternity. When I put people together, it's normally until death. But there are rare cases when the couple loves each other SOOO much that they really want eternity. I said in my word that when a couple dies, they are like the angels. Neither marrying nor given in marriage. But there is something eternal about true love. The love I create does not die when one of them does. That love is eternal. It may take on another form, but it is eternal."

_ * _

Gregg walked into the place on the 21st. He looked across the room, and Jean was standing there smiling at him. He melted. He knew that she was sent by the Father. He walked across the room over to her. He touched her hand and smiled.

Jean blushed. She knew there was something special about Gregg. She just did not totally understand what, but she knew she had to find out.

Gregg looked into her beautiful brown eyes and smiled and said. "Jean, it's really a pleasure to get to know you. Have you been a lifelong resident of this community?"

Jean smiled. "I have, and where might you be from, my friend.?"

Gregg could not help but smile. "I am from a little hamlet called Merilyn Wisconsin. Born and raised there. Went to the university in Wisconsin and now got drafted by Dallas. I am trying to get used to this southern hospitality. I must say northern people are not nearly as friendly."

"Mr. Gregg, tell me, why football? To be honest, I am not a big sports nut. I enjoy a game from time to time, but nothing at the fanatic level. Why football?" She asked.

"It's like this; we are all given gifts. Those gifts may be something big or small. I don't know if being able to run extremely fast and catch a football is considered big or not, but that's what I have been given. You see, it's not how big our gift is; it's how hard are we willing to work to accomplish what the Father has created us to do. I am doing just that. I use my gifts to accomplish what the Father has created me to do. You see, I use my gifts to open doors to be reaching people who might not be able to be reached in any other way. Being a star football player has a way of opening doors."

Jean could not help but smile. She was looking at a very gifted athlete. She could see his love for people through their brief conversation, especially kids. This touched her heart in ways that she did not expect. "If he loves kids that much, how much more will he love his own?" Was the thought that was going through her mind. She could feel the excitement for this new guy in her life she had not felt with anyone else. She knew she had to really get to know this guy.

The next day at practice, Coach Wolf, the receiver coach, pulled Tommy and Gregg aside. "You two are probably the greatest receiving tandem the sport of football has ever seen. We never know how long we will keep great players together in this league. So, we will go all out this season and play a reckless form of football. We will play like there is no tomorrow because there might not be.

Gregg smiled. "Coach Wolf, I don't know where you are at concerning Christ, but you have just spoken a truth that should resonate through the whole community of Christ. None of us knows how much time we have left on this earth. We need to live every moment like it's our last. We need to not hold back but pour ourselves into everything we are doing like our last day on this earth. For all we know, it could be."

Tommy looked at Gregg. "My friend, you do realize this is going to be a whole lot of work, but boy, is it gonna be fun!" Gregg was beginning to see the value of a sport called 23: with that, both men headed for their lockers to get ready for practice that day.

- * -

Tommy

The Father said. "Pete, do you realize what I am doing here. You see, I connected with Eli, Jill, and Tommy. I did that for a couple of reasons. But also realize this, I have placed Gregg with Tommy at Dallas for a reason. That reason is this. I will touch millions of kids through the foundation they will start after this season. That foundation will be set up to help student-athletes who are not at the level that I have, Tommy and Greg. But they have a love for the sport. I will use these two young men to reach these kids and introduce the kids to my Son Jesus. They are going to use the gifts I have given them to a great advantage for my kingdom."

_ * _

The first game of the regular season was against Minnesota. Tommy arranged box seats for Eli and his whole family. Herman would be in the stands watching Tommy catch one touchdown and Gregg catches two. Herman looked over at his dad Eli and said. "Dad, someday I will be throwing touchdown passes to Tommy. I can feel it; I think he can too. After all, mom gave us both life. We owe it to her to be a great tandem."

Jill looked at her son Herman. She smiled and said. "Hermie, first, you have to get drafted. To get drafted, you must be an outstanding player in college. Then you must make the pro team. Then if Tommy is not on your team, the team you are on would have to trade for him; in other words, it will take a miracle."

Herman could only smile as he watched, in his mind, Tommy catches his touchdown pass. "Mom, we serve the Great I am; I believe that God our Father through His Son Jesus has a reason for us to play together. I don't know what that reason is, but there is a reason. We will find out in due time. Remember what you always told me. When the time is right, things happen."

_ * _

The Father looked at Peter. "Pete, I love it when my kids get it. Herman gets it. It's not the great work they do on the football field that is the reason I created them. Their football prowess is for what happens after they are both done with the game. They will be extraordinarily rich men. Yet the lives they touch will be more for the kids than when they were active in the game. You see, Pete, I use events in people's lives to build their testimony that other people can relate to positively. When that happens, people open up in ways that will allow my servants to reach into their hearts with the power of My Holy Spirit in ways that will amaze them."

_ * _

Throughout the regular season, the tandem of Tommy and Gregg would catch touchdown pass after touchdown pass. 15 opposing teams would fall to Dallas as the season went on. Then the Playoffs, flat does not even come close to describing just how the emotion of going undefeated during the regular season and the feeling of being invincible would set them up to be taken out in the first game. Playing Atlanta for the first time that season, who had lost only one game, and they're taking them for granted, caused their ultimate defeat. Falling behind by twenty in the first quarter would be impossible to overcome. Even Tommy and Gregg catching a touchdown pass a piece was not enough to overcome the huge deficit that the defence had left them in. Both men would pour everything into the game that they had left, the quarterback would hit them with pinpoint passes, but their defense just could not stop the Atlanta machine. After the game, they would sit in their locker room for an hour in silence. The whole team just looked at each other and tried to figure out what had happened.

Then the coach walked in. "Gentlemen, this season has been one for the books. Upper management has assured me that this team will be kept together for at least one more year. That should allow us another year to pull off that big win. After that, we will see what happens." Coach Wolf turned and walked out with that, leaving his team to lick their wounds.

Gregg and Tommy looked at each other, wondering if their goal of having that Superbowl ring would come to fruition. They both felt like crying. Then the thought hit them both at the same time. "Tommy spoke first. This is a game. A game, nothing more, nothing less. This game gives us a platform to speak into kids' lives. We must use that platform to accomplish what the Father has in store for us. We must use that platform to be the men our Father in heaven has created us to be for such a time as this. I remember when I first saw Eli McBrien. He was sitting with his bride. The smile on his face when I walked over to them was amazing. That's when Sharon donated her bone marrow to me, saving my life so he could use me in this game, only emphasizing the importance of doing as much with the gifts I have been given as I can. I must accomplish the most I can with them. And we must be able to reach kids with these gifts. Our gifts will open doors to kids' hearts that would not be able to be opened otherwise." Tommy said.

During the offseason, both men got active in different churches around town. Both men would lead the respective youth groups in the churches The Father of all mankind directed them to. A couple of the young men in the youth groups, from separate groups, knew each other. They got together in school and came up with a flag football game between the two churches. Gregg called Tommy.

"Hey bro, you suppose we should see if we can start a church league for flag football. It just may be fun?" Gregg asked.

Tommy could not help but smile. He remembered Eli telling stories about playing bible baseball with the kids from First Church and the Catholic church he was a member of. He was just wondering how they could work the scripture into flag football. He knew Jesus would be in the middle of the whole thing. "Gregg, when Eli McBrien and Sam Boursa played together for LA, they created a game called bible baseball as an Icebreaker for getting their youth groups off the ground. They would set up questions for singles, doubles, triples, and home runs. My question is this, how do we make flag football something that can bring the word of God to these kids we are dealing with?" Tommy asked.

The look on Gregg's face was one of bewilderment. "Bro, to be honest, I have no idea, but I am sure that the Father, through His Son Jesus by His Holy Spirit, put that thought in your heart. Let's both go home, spend the night praying about this and see what the Father has." Gregg answered.

_ * _

All the Father had to say to Peter was, "Watch this."

_ * _

The next day Tommy woke with an idea; 'I think we should not tie flag football directly to a competition that will have the effect of one

Christian group against the other. Instead, why not have both teams meet in the middle of the field, just before the coin toss, spend time in prayer for safety and good sportsmanship. Then have the coin toss, and then we let the competition begin. After all, this is a church league flag football, is it not? 'Tommy then picked up the phone and got ahold of Gregg and shared his ideas with him.

The next week the competition will begin. Both teams were chomping at the bit to get going with the games. Then the joint prayer before the game. Suddenly, both teams were willing to go at it, but the feelings of animosity were gone. The competition was still there at an extremely high level, but both teams realized that they were playing against brothers in the Lord, and they had to treat each other with the respect they deserved.

The score was kept, both teams played their hearts out, and both wanted to join in prayer after the game. Both teams joined each other at Tom Lipinski's Dairy Queen to celebrate after the game. The teams did not remember who won or lost, but they enjoyed their Peanut Buster Parfaits and Blizzards as they joked and laughed after the game. They all had a great time.

The rest of the offseason came and went quickly. Katie, Jon, and Tommy took a trip to the gulf coast for a mini-vacation in June just before the season started. They needed the time to unwind and be a family before the season would start. Tommy realized that alone as a family would be a rare thing once the season started. This little getaway to the gulf coast would give them the time just to be. They would not have to worry about the press or any pressure from anyone for 4 days. Just a bit of time to sit back and go AHHHHHHHHHH. But the season was quickly approaching, and they had to be ready.

10. SEASON TWO OF THE TOMMY AND GREGG SHOW

Season two of the Tommy and Gregg show would turn out to be magical. From the beginning of the pre-season until the end of the season, these two speedsters would prove to be too much of a challenge for just about every team in the league. The season opener would be played against Minnesota. Minnesota had been dealing with a quarterback controversy ever since last year. They played one quarterback one week and another the next. They even tried trading for a quarterback mid-season last year, trying to fill the hole that just seemed to get deeper and deeper. They just could not seem to get a really great fit in that key position. It was almost as if God the Father had planned and kept that position open.

In the meantime, Herman was tearing up the league as a high school quarterback. Some of the passes he was completing were blowing away all the sportswriters around the country.

_ * _

Pete, what I have planned is teaching the world a lesson on my timing. I am going to show them that my timing is always perfect. I have planned this whole affair for hundreds of years. I had to put the genetics together perfectly for this whole thing to come about. The tools I give one person are a mix of things I started a thousand years ago. It excites me to no end to see my kids take the gifts they have been given and use them in such a way that more and more people are drawn into my kingdom.

_ * _

Tommy

Tommy and Gregg were walking outside the stadium. Gregg looked at Tommy. "Man, it's like this. We are both here because many people poured into our lives. I can think of one pastor who really poured into my life. He would hear me out on many things, give some input to me, and then we would go our separate ways. Tommy remembers this. You and I have been given lots of talent that, over time, will diminish. We are both at the top of our careers with speed to burn. Let's see, you're about 25, and I am 23, fresh out of college. We have both graduated with degrees and will have life after football, but the question is, what are we going to be doing? I can run a 3.9 forty right now, you are not quite that fast, but you still burn it. As time goes on, we both know that speed will diminish. Like the old farmer said, we must make hey while the sun shines. That is what our whole lives must be. Wherever the Lord sends us after football, we must work like no tomorrow because there may not be a tomorrow.

Tommy's facial expression was one of concern. "We are both working for a huge business. The money we make here can be used to see thousands of lives changed. Planning for our future is something we both need to be concerned with. But we must be concerned with the here and now as well. I would say this. Let's be focused on one game at a time. We need to make each play count. That play could be sharing the gospel with many young football players, or it could be catching a touchdown pass from a great quarterback. Either way, we will have one shot at that play we make. There are no repeats in life. We make it count now, for there is no tomorrow."

That night Tommy gave Herman a call. "Hey there, young man, I here you tore things up this last season starting your sophomore year on the varsity football team. Is that correct?" Tommy asked.

"Pretty much!" Was Herman's answer. "I feel like I am doing what I was created to do." He continued.

Tommy got a grin on his face. "You are correct; you were created to play football. You can take all of the fame and fortune that will come with it, or you can use it to further the kingdom of God our Father and see more and more kids come to an understanding of who Jesus really is. High school would be a great place to start with the ministry end of it." Tommy continued.

Herman looked a bit forlorn. "Mr. Tommy, I would love to throw passes to you. There are SOOO many years between us. You will probably be retired before I even get to where I might get drafted." He said.

Tommy chuckled." Hermey, there would be truly little that would excite me more. But this I do know, if our Father in heaven needs to team us up for one team or another, he will do it. We both must maintain a high level of play to have any hope of that happening. And that level of play does not matter what team we play for. As Rush Limbaugh used to say, we have been given talent,' on loan from God.' We must, I mean we must continue to push ourselves to be the best at whatever we do to accomplish what the Father through His Son Jesus by His Holy Spirit has for us to do."

Herman, holding his phone close to his ear, started to feel the excitement running through him. "Mr. Tommy, you are starting your third year, if I am right?" he asked.

"That is right," Tommy answered.

"I have 1 more year of High School ball, then 4 years of college; I have to get drafted. I don't know if I can accomplish all of that?" Herman said.

Tommy had to ask a question that would keep Herman motivated for the next five years." How bad do you want it?" He asked Herman.

Herman blinked a bit. "Mr. Tommy, I am not a real patient person; when I want something, I want it right now. But in this instance, I know it will be all in God the Father's timing."

Tommy spoke directly to Herman. "Herman, know this, our Father's timing is always perfect. When I was working on a project I did not know if it would ever come about, I heard the Holy Spirit speak to me. One little phrase was all it took to give me the patients that I really needed when I needed it. "When the time is right, things happen." I used that repeatedly as I went through some really trying times. I never gave up but kept on it until the task was completed. My young friend, that is exactly what I feel you must keep telling yourself as you go through this ordeal. You need to keep your grades up. You need to be that student that all the other kids look up to. Herman high school and college will be some great times for you. Don't rush to get out but enjoy every moment. You will not get another shot at life. You will never have another shot at high school or college sports, for that matter. You will find your first love in high school. Treat her like the princess that she was created to be. Enjoy being the 'big' man on campus. That will disappear when you hit college. Remember, when the time is right, things happen.

Herman smiled as Tommy could hear the excitement building within him. "Mr. Tommy, I will keep working; I will accomplish what the Father through the Son by His Spirit has created me to do. I will be the best quarterback that I can be. Where The Father takes me will be an exciting ride. I am excited to be the best God has created me to be!" Herman stated with absolute authority.

Tommy hung up the phone. He sat back on the leather office chair next to his desk. He looked to Heaven and prayed quietly. "Father, you have given me two great young men to get to where you want them. One is Herman, and the other is my Son by another dad. You gave me Jon to raise as my son, thank you. Father, I beg of you to make me the man who can help both these young men you gave me the men you want them to be. You gave Herman a great dad who has done an amazing job. Eli McBrien must be a great dad to raise a son of Herman's quality. Jonathon looks to be an amazing young man. Thank you for giving him his dad for just a bit to be that person who could speak into his son's life and get the message that you have placed me in his life. In Jesus' name, please? Amen."

Tommy then picked up the phone again and dialed Gregg. "Hey, Gregg, when was the last time you were at a high school football game?"

"Oh, the last game I was at was in my senior year of High School. I played in it. Scored 4 touchdowns. Why do you ask?" Gregg asked Herman.

"We have a bye week in two weeks. I could keep Jonathon out of school on Friday, and we could make it a guy's trip. What do you say we fly up to Carlton, Minnesota, and see Herman McBrien play quarterback for the Carlton Bulldogs? What do you think?"

Gregg got a smile on his face. "You know, bro, that may not be a bad idea. Let's do it. Let's touch base with the school and see if maybe we can meet the team before the game and give them a real motivational speech."

Tommy nodded as he said. "I will call the coach of the team. We won't tell the guys we are coming, so it will be a real surprise for them." With that, Tommy hung up and dialed Carlton High School to talk to the coach.

"This is Carlton High School; May I help you?" The school secretary said as she answered the phone.

"This is Tommy Richardson; I play football for Dallas. Is your football coach in?" Tommy asked.

Jim Erickson came to the phone. "This is Jim Erickson; I am the football coach here."

This is Tommy Richardson, with Dallas. Gregg Shoemaker and I will be in your area next Friday night. This is our bye week, and you have a young quarterback named Herman McBrien. You see, Coach, I am alive because of his mom. Jill McBrien. I had leukemia, and she donated bone marrow to become the player I am today. Any chance we could surprise the team during your speech before the game?"

Jim got a look, hoping this was not a scam of some sort. "You guys are telling the truth, aren't you?" He asked them.

"Tell you what, Mr. Erickson, why not have Hermey come to the phone and let me confirm that I am telling the truth."

Mrs. Anderson, the school secretary, looked up Herman's class. She then paged him to the office. He walked in and saw the coach on the phone. Coach Erickson then handed the phone the Herman and had him say hello.

"Mr. Tommy, It's so good to hear your voice. What that's all you had me called here to do was verify who you are. What a bummer. Now I can go back to class. See me soon. How soon?" Hermey asked.

With that, he handed to phone back to Coach Erickson. "Now, do you believe me?" Tommy said.

"See you soon." The coach responded as he smiled and said good-bye."

The next Friday, they landed in Duluth, rented a new Challenger, and drove over to the school. They walked into the office, and Coach Erickson was called. They would spend the next hour going over the offence that the Bulldogs would be using that night. That night they would walk into the locker room and look at the young studs getting ready for their game. The look on the players' faces made the trip totally worthwhile. Coach Erickson walked in. "Men, I would like to introduce you to Gregg Shoemaker and Tommy Richardson from Dallas. They have come to watch you play tonight. Gentlemen, would you like to address the team?" Coach Erickson asked Gregg and Tommy.

Tommy walked to the podium. "Gentlemen, you have all been given gifts from our Father in heaven. I would like to pose an open question to each of you. What is your responsibility with the gifts you have been given?"

Kevin Derusha raised his hand. "Mr. Tommy, my responsibility with the gifts I have been given is to drive the opposing running back into the ground. My job is to cause as much damage to the opposing running back on the first hit as I can, so he does not want to run into the side of the field that it is my job to protect our goal line from the opposition. When I am running the football, my job is to either run away from the guys who want to stop me or run over them and just keep on going." He said with a smile.

Coach Erickson walked over to Tommy and whispered into his ear.

"Tommy, I know you would like to expand on that question. It's a great question. I need these guys thinking about this game. You have got them fired up. Let's talk more about this after the game."

Tommy smiled as he said. "You got it, coach."

The game would prove brutal as Herman would throw a couple of touchdown passes. Tommy walked over to Colin Irvin during halftime, the tall wide receiver for the Bulldogs. "Say, Colin, their corner has you tied up in knots. Here's what you do. Next time you fake in, give a quick step like you're going out, then cut in hard. That throws me off every time."

Irvin walked into the huddle. Herman looked directly at him as he called the play. "93 slant reverse on three."

The team ran to the line. Herman crouched down under center and called the play. On the third "Go," they lit up the field. Irvin ran the route just as Tommy suggested he run it. He would suddenly find himself wide open, turn on the afterburners. Herman would see his wide open and throw a perfect pass that would drop into his hands for a touchdown. The crowd would go wild with excitement. Herman and Irvin would find themselves the Heroes of the game.

Final score: 28-21 Carlton.

After the game, Tommy and Gregg walked into the locker room. Coach Erickson gave Tommy the nod to follow up on his question before the game. As the young men walked into the locker room, they greeted both Tommy and Gregg. That sat down tired but elated over their victory. Tommy spoke first. "Gentlemen, you won a good victory tonight. However, we need to keep this in the perspective of the whole. Let's ask this question. What difference does this one game make in the big picture? What difference does it make in the scope of tomorrow? Probably not a whole lot, or does it? In a couple of years, things are going bad on something you are trying to work on. You think back to being down by a touchdown with less than a minute to play. That guy across from you on the line has been beating you up all night. You think to yourself, 'I dug deep then, found the strength, and got the victory, I can do it again.' That, my friends, is what you learned tonight. You have all been given gifts. The question in the big scheme of things is, what are you going to do with your gifts? The question is, why did God the Father, through His Son Jesus by the Holy Spirit, give you the gifts he did? Are you going to waste them, or will you translate them into something that will carry you through the rest of your life? Are you going to use your gifts to change people's lives for the better? Remember this, there is life after football. We must accomplish all that we can while we play, but this short time will end. We each will have that last game. Whether in High School, College, or Professional, all sports careers end. The question is this. Are you ready to play with all your heart at whatever level the Lord sees fit to use you in? Are you ready to use those gifts to touch lives when you are done? Gentlemen, the choice is yours." With that, he looked over to coach Erickson and nodded and smiled.

Greg Donaldson looked at the two pro stars and had to ask a question. "We are all going to the junction out on Highway 210. Would you guys like to join us?"

Tommy looked at Gregg. Both men smiled at the same time. "Gregg, where was your spot after every game in high school?" Tommy asked.

"Gregg smiled. "It was Sam's place in Black River Falls. We would spend a couple of hours after every game. I think this could be a lot of fun!"

They walked out, got into the Challenger that they had rented, and followed the rest of the team out to the junction. As they walked into the Junction, they expected everyone to go GAGA over them. But then they realized they were in northern Minnesota, not Texas, where everyone would recognize them. Tommy looked at Gregg and said. "This is cool, kinda like going back to high school ball. We are not a big deal. Kinda cool, eh!"

Gregg chuckled as he looked around, and the other students were making a big deal about Herman, and his three touchdown passes. Kevin Derusha was walking around slapping all his buddies on the back; Lute Mullenix was sitting in his usual booth with his girlfriend Debbie holding hands. One could look at how they looked at each other what they had in mind. Yup, the same old stuff; high school never changes, all the students had a role, and they played it well.

None of the students even noticed the professional football hero's in their midst. All they knew was that the Carlton Bulldogs had just one huge game, and the kids were going to celebrate the great victory...

At that second, Peter Reed noticed the Challenger outside the window. "Who belongs to that car?" He asked.

Gregg stood up. "That belongs to me; at least it's my rental." He answered.

"And who might you be?" Pete asked.

"I am Gregg Shoemaker. My friend here is Tommy Henderson."

No one on the Bulldog team would say anything about them playing for Dallas. The time they were having was one of these players just being part of the gang. The team just wanted them to enjoy themselves without the rest of the Junction going nuts because a couple of famous players were there eating.

"These are just a couple of friends of my family who came to see the game. Gregg and Tommy."

At that moment, John Anderson spoke up. "You guys look familiar. Where are you from?"

"Oh, here and there." That was the answer that Tommy gave. The two pro players did not want to really give that information away.

Reed would not be shaken off by these two guys. "You look really familiar. Come on. Tell us where you are from?!"

"Aren't you, Tommy Richardson? You played for Carlton, a bunch of years ago. I think you play for Dallas now?" Reed asked.

"You got me. We both play for Dallas. I have been following Herman since he was a freshman. I think this kid has some real talent and will go far." Tommy said.

Jonathon looked at his dad. "Dad, I would love a burger. I am starved."

Tommy waved the waitress over. "What can I get you, young man?" Kerry, the waitress, asked.

"How about that double bacon cheeseburger up there. I am starved?"

Kerry smiled. "Will do, champ, coming right up," She said.

Gregg added. "We flew up to watch him play, the rest of the team as well, but we focused on him. Let me say this. You can have the greatest quarterback in the world; if he does not have a great team surrounding him, he goes nowhere. One thing that was evident tonight, he had a great team around him."

Herman was smiling ear to ear. He knew he had a bright future was in front of him. He just knew it would be big. He knew it involved football and that God's greatness would shine through him. He just had no idea what that would look like. He just did not understand what The Father through the Son by the Spirit had in mind.

11. ADVENTURE ON THE FLIGHT BACK

The next morning Tommy and Gregg were woken early. They hopped down to the Challenger and headed for the airport in Minneapolis. As they drove down, they could not help but talk about young Herman and how he looked to have a lot of potential for a college quarterback, possibly even the pros. As they were cruising down the freeway, they noticed a car broke down on the side of the road. They noticed a young lady standing outside the car. They pulled over being the gentlemen they were, more than willing to help a damsel in distress. As they pulled up, the beautiful blonde got a worried look on her face.

Tommy walked up to the young lady and asked her what the problem was. "Who are you guys?" She asked.

I am Tommy Richardson; this is Gregg Shoemaker; I am a wide receiver. Gregg is a tailback. We both play for Dallas." Was Tommy's response.

"I just got this car. It just quit running." Tommy smiled. He asked permission to sit in her car. The young lady granted it. He hopped in, put the key in the ignition, and turned it. The car started right up. The young lady's face turned bright red. "I don't understand this. Could you guys follow me to the airport? I have to pick up my dad?" She asked them.

Gregg being the single one in the group, smiled and said. "Young lady, we are at your service. If you would like, I would love to ride down with you?"

She got a look on her face that said, "Help!"

Tommy smiled; if you would be uncomfortable with that, there is no problem. Gregg is safe, we are both committed believers in Christ, and I know that sex outside of marriage is something that Gregg does not believe in."

Just then, the young lady spoke up. The look on Gregg's face was one of total surprise. He knew that Tommy was well aware of his faith in Christ, but he had never talked to him about his views on pre-marital sex.

"Gregg, is that true? You see, I am also committed to Christ, and those are my beliefs as well. Do you really believe that?"

Gregg had thoughts going through his mind. He had to decide on the spot what he really did believe on the subject. He had never thought about it much as he was shy in high school. In college, the girls came onto him. But his shyness would always get the better of him. He had trouble understanding why he had even asked this beautiful young lady if she would like him to ride with her, and he hadn't even asked her what her name was. "Before I answer that question, let me ask you one question, what is your name."

She smiled at Gregg. "My name is Jessica; my friends call me Jessie."

Gregg smiled. "Jessie, it's like this, all through school, both high school and college, I was very shy. To be honest, that question had never crossed my mind. I know that celibacy before marriage is God the Father through His Son Jesus by His Holy Spirits best. I have always wanted God's best. Therefore, let's just say that that is what I believe as well."

Jessie smiled at Gregg. "I think I am going to trust you. But for extra safety on my part, you drive. That way, I don't have to worry about things, and we can take the time to get to know each other. When you get to the airport, you will even get to meet my Father."

Gregg stopped in his tracks. He had not dated many girls and had never met any of their Father. He looked to heaven and smiled and prayed for The Father's guidance on the whole thing. They had a great conversation during the ninety-minute drive to the airport. Jessie's dad was standing outside the terminal as they pulled up, waiting. Gregg pulled over and stepped out of the car, walked around, and opened the door for Jessie. Gregg held out his hand and greeted her dad. "My name is Gregg Shoemaker."

Her dad took Gregg's hand. "Howard Jones here; I see you have met my daughter. You helped her when her car stalled on the freeway, correct?" Howard asked.

Gregg looked at Jessie. "Did you call him?" Gregg asked.
"Nope, I did not," Jessie replied.

Howard looked at the couple. "When I was flying here from Dallas, I felt like I needed to pray. I prayed that Jessie's car would stop running and that her future husband would stop and rescue her. So, have you two talked about a wedding?" He asked.
Both Gregg and Jessies faces became red as beats. "Daddy, what are you talking about?" Jessie asked.

"Jessie, meet your husband, Gregg, meet your wife; all we need to know is a minister, and we can put this whole thing together," Howard stated.

With that, Jessie called her mom. "Mom, we are picking dad up at the airport. Something strange is going on here. I just met this guy. He tells me that he prayed I would break down on the road on his way back from Dallas, and my husband would come along and help me out. Now he wants to set a wedding date. I am not ready to set a wedding date, Jessie said to her mom with emotions that surprised her.

Gregg looked at Tommy. "We have got a plane to catch to get back to Dallas. We have practice tomorrow." Gregg stated, almost pleading.
Tommy smiled. "Naaa, we have three hours until plane our leaves; take your time." He said with a smile on his face. He thought, 'Get yourself out of this one hot shot.'
Tommy looked at Howard, "Howard, I have an idea. Why doesn't Jessie fly down for next week's game? She can stay with my bride Sharon and I. Let's give them a chance to get to know each other. If this is the will of the Father, he will work out the relational parts of it between the two of them. I am sure that Gregg here can afford to buy her a ticket."
Howard got a look on his face that said. "I am thinking about it." He turned and walked a few steps towards the terminal. Then he turned back. "Ok, that makes sense to me."
Gregg walked the few steps to get close to Jessie. "I can't believe this is happening. What if this is what the Father through the Son by

the Spirit planned for us all along. What then?"

Jessie turned toward Gregg. "Gregg, give me a hug." Gregg smiled and hugged her tight, then he felt her kiss his cheek.

Gregg smiled. "Jessie, there's something here. I think we need to explore this and see where it goes. If the Father can 'arrange' to have Tommy's life saved by a "chance" meeting in a restaurant, I think he could arrange a marriage by using your car that was not really broken down. What do you think?" He asked.

Jessie smiled. "Ok, you get my ticket, and I will see you next weekend. Here is my phone number." She pulled a notepad from her purse and gave her number to Gregg.

Jessie hopped into the car with her dad, Gregg and Tommy walked into the airport. They checked their bags and found their seats in first class. As they sat there, the look on Greggs's face was one of bewilderment and wonder. "What just happened. I see God's hand all over this. Yet I wonder what the rest of my life would be like with this woman that I don't even know?

Tommy smiled. "Gregg, you know there is only one way you are going to find out. That is to pray for the next couple of weeks, work your butt off on the football field, and off the field you go into seclusion and seek the Father's face through His Son Jesus by the Holy Spirit as to whether or not this whole thing is of him."

The couple behind them could not help but overhear. "Excuse me, gentlemen. I am the pastor of First Church in Dallas. If I am not mistaken, you both play for Dallas, is that correct?" The pastor asked.

Tommy spoke up. "It is. Are you a fan?""

The pastor's wife smiled. "I am going to guess that something happened totally out of the ordinary. Something you would not have seen coming in a million years. Is that correct?"

Gregg chuckled a bit. "You could say that." He answered.

"Then you really need to seek the face of God our Father through His Son Jesus by this Holy Spirit and see if what happened is really supposed to happen; if yes, then pour yourself into it a hundred percent." The pastor's wife said.

"If I do, it will change the path of my life forever," Gregg answered.

The pastor's wife smiled. "Care to share with me what happened?" She asked.

Gregg would spend the next 20 minutes sharing with the couple in front of them what happened on the trip down, including what Jessie's dad told them at the airport. The pastor's wife smiled as she asked this question. "Mr. Gregg, what if this really was a God thing, and this young lady is supposed to be your helpmate for the rest of your life? What if God the Father has planned the sons and daughters you two are supposed to have for some special work in His kingdom?" The pastor's wife asked.

Gregg looked at Mrs. Pastor. "Then, mam, life is going to get very interesting." He said, smiling. But all of this is dependent on my decision whether I am going to take this leap of faith, is it not? He asked.

_*_

The next week at practice, Gregg was hitting on all cylinders. He not only was going to impress the crowd that would out to see him, but he was also making sure his game would be such that Jessie would be thoroughly impressed with his athletic ability. His plan was to blow away all the defensive backs and score as many touchdowns as he possibly could to impress this young lady. His mind was not centered on impressing a young lady this much since high school.

_*_

Jessie walked into the Kitchen. "Daddy, did you really pray that my car would break down, and my next husband would be the one to stop and help me?"

Her dad, Dr. Johnson, smiled a big toothy grin. "Young lady, I sure did; I was on the plain talking to the person next to me. It was like I heard this voice telling me to pray that prayer. I was almost blown away when I saw you in the car with Gregg Shoemaker. I could hardly believe it." He said.

"Wait a minute. You knew who Gregg was?"

"I sure did. I have been a Dallas fan for years. That kid is faster than grease lightning. I could not have planned this myself?" The doc. Said.

"Daddy, what if he had been just a regular guy. Would you have told him about the prayer?"

I would have had to. I trust the Father's plans. They are always better than mine. I have been trusting him ever since I was a kid. Look where It got me."

Jessie smiled at her dad. "Daddy, you know I trust you. You know I also trust God. Don't know if I would have had the faith to pray that prayer, but I do trust God." At that second, her phone rang. "Hello, this is Jessie."

"Jessie, I would love to have you fly down this weekend and see our game against Minnesota; your dad is welcome as well, although he is buying his own ticket," Gregg said.

She looked at her dad. "Daddy, Gregg has invited us both down for the weekend to see Dallas play Minnesota. He does say you have to buy your own ticket. Interested?"

The Doctor was smiling ear to ear. "I guess I can afford my own ticket." He said, chuckling.

The following weekend they flew down. That weekend would prove to be magical. They would dine in the finest restaurant Saturday night. Sunday Gregg would catch 3 touchdown passes. Tommy would take a reverse and run for another. Dallas would blow Minnesota out 53 to 7. The good doctor would be in 7th Heaven thinking about having this guy for a son and the grandkids they would be giving him.

Sitting beside her dad in the stands, Jessie asked her dad. "Daddy penny for your thoughts?"

The Doc smiled. "Just thinking about the grandkids, you kids could give me." He said.

"Oh, Daddy!" Jessie said with a face getting red with embarrassment.

The Doc could not help but chuckle. He looked at his daughter and smiled, then he chuckled, then he broke out into a full belly laugh. "You guys will make me some amazing grandkids."

The game was over; Jessie and her dad were waiting outside the stadium for Tommy and Gregg to come out. As Gregg walked out of the gate, he looked at Jessie and started to melt inside. He looked up to heaven and mouthed the words. "Thank you." He knew in his heart that this woman was the one the Father had planned for him for thousands of years. He knew that the Father of all mankind had something special in mind when he answered her father's prayer and the car broke down. It was not until the flight back to Dallas that he would open up with Tommy about his feelings.

Tommy looked at Gregg. "You do understand now what the scripture meant when it said A good wife who can find? Do you not. I mean, look who wrote it. An incredibly wise man. Solomon."

The smile on Greggs's face was wide and bright. Tommy then broke into Gregg's world. "My friend. We have a game to play. Get your head into it. You will be playing for the first time in front of Jessie. Make it good!" That did get Gregg's head in the game. The score would show just how into the game he was. The adventures of Jessie and Gregg were just starting. Gregg would be a show-off. Scoring big and making the defensive backs look foolish. But it was early in the season. And Jessie having a pro football player for a fiancé was good for her ego.

After the game, Jessie and Gregg went out to dinner at the End Zone nightclub in town. It was the first time they could be on the town with just the two of them. As they walked into the restaurant part of the club, Jessie smiled. She had her arm through Gregg's, and her step did not just bounce; each step about threw her to the ceiling. She was so excited. The hostess seated them across the table from them. Abby, the waitress, liked waiting on Gregg. He was a huge tipper.

Abby sensed this night would be something special for the two love birds. It was as if this little voice was telling her to do everything; she could make the evening something special for the two people in front of her that could not take their eyes off each other.

They sat at the table and touched their fingers together. As they touched, one could almost see the sparks flowing from their fingertips like one would see on a spark plug. The electricity being exchanged between them as they looked into one another's eyes was as if they had known each other for years; what they were feeling was quite evident.

As Gregg walked into the practice facility on Monday, he was almost floating on air. That would end shortly. On the first play of practice, a reverse was called. John James, the right linebacker, saw Gregg flying toward him from the left. John moved up into the backfield and dropped him like a hot rock. John looked down on Gregg as he stood over him. "Shoemaker, I would suggest you get your head in the game. That new little sweety of yours is going to have one busted-up boyfriend if you don't." With that, he turned and walked away from Gregg.

Gregg played like a man on fire for the rest of the practice. He outran out, jumped, and outscored the rest of the team. When he got into his home, he picked up the phone and called Jessie. "Sweetheart, during the season, I will see you only after the game. I must keep my eye on the prize here. I have a whole team counting on me to do my part. One team member does not perform to his full capacity, the whole team can suffer and lose. We really don't want that to happen."

Jessie held her phone from her deepest part and wanted to see Gregg more than Sunday after a game. She knew that it was not a wise and selfish thing to happen. She realized that Gregg was also being paid millions of dollars a year and had to play at his peak to earn that money. She knew he had performance bonuses built into his contract. He had to operate at his full potential to get that money. Jessie knew she could not stand in the way of him accomplishing everything that lay before him. In the back of her mind, she knew that her future was also involved.

The season went by quickly for Gregg. He wanted more than Sunday afternoons as well. But he realized that he had to keep his head in the game. Their future depended on it. He would not risk their future for anything. He had to keep his head in the game. Win after win, game after game, drew them to the Superbowl and the end of the season. After the season was over, they could relax and spend time enjoying each other after they won another Superbowl. Then Gregg did it. He had talked to her Father and got permission first. The first Friday after the season, Gregg took Jessie to the nicest restaurant in Dallas. Over desert, he stood up, walked over to where she was sitting, got down on one knee, and pulled out a ring that was so bright they almost had to dim the lights in the restaurant.

Gregg asked her to be his bride; when she came out of the chair and threw her arms around his neck, she about knocked him over. Her smile was so broad, everyone in the place could hear her scream. 'Yes, Yes, Yes! As they walked out of the restaurant holding hands, she could hear congratulations from every table. Jessie was flying with excitement as they were leaving. Her smile just kept getting broader and broader.

Gregg and Jessie would take the next weekend and drive to see her dad. Her Dad had only one question for Gregg. "Why did you wait so long to ask the question that you know you wanted to from the first time you saw her?"

At this point, Gregg found himself getting a bit "ticked" off with Jessie's dad. The thoughts went through his mind. "How dare he, this man may have a good connection with the Father through the Son by the Spirit, but he is completely lacking in-tact." "Sir, I believe in following God's timing is everything. During the season was not his timing. I do respect you as your beautiful daughter's father. However, you need to learn something called tact." Gregg answered.

Doctor Johnson smiled. "One thing I like about this young man is he is willing to stand for those things he believes are right. Gregg, I have learned that the best way to deal with things is head-on in my profession. People need to know the truth. You will always know where I am coming from; I also need to know exactly what is going on with you. I can see that will not be a problem. I can see we are going to get along just fine. I do believe in God's timing. I also know that he started planning your kids getting together hundreds of years ago. The one thing to keep in mind is this. When your kids come along, and they will, each of those kids has a role in the Father's big plan. Your role as parents is to nurture that child so that when the Father through His Son Jesus by His Holy Spirit reveals it, the child is prepared to function in the role that the Father has laid out for them.

"So, what I hear you saying is this. God has our roles set; we have no choice in what we end up doing?" Gregg asked.

"Not at all, people are created, and they have choices through their life. They can choose to follow God's best, or they can choose to do things their way and see where things work out. I think following the plan that the Father has planned is going to make life a great adventure, and you have to admit, the retirement plan is not bad either."

Gregg smiled as he said. "Dr. Johnson, I can guarantee this; the kids God brings into this family are going to be raised in the fear and admonition of the Lord. They will be raised that the talents they have been given are a gift of the Father, and because of that, they must work their butts off accomplishing all they can for the kingdom."

The good Doctor smiled to himself. He knew that Gregg was a man of honor and would follow through on his promise. He also knew that the legacy he had started with his daughter would carry on forever. He also knew that his Father in heaven had a plan. This plan started hundreds of years prior, if not thousands. He knew he would have to put the right people together to have this couple for such a time as this. He knew that he had to support these kids in a way that would get them into the positions that the Father through the Son by the Spirit wanted them in to accomplish what the Father had for them to accomplish. He knew the Father's goal was to bring more and more of his kids to himself. He knew that the kids who were totally sold out to his purpose could be counted on as his messengers to get his message of salvation by His Son Jesus, who paid the ultimate sacrifice on Good Friday out to the world. He also knew that the salvation of generations to come would be dependent on the kids of this day growing and teaching their kids of the salvation that the Father was offering through the sacrifice of his Son Jesus on the Cross.

12. THE GREGG AND TOMMY SHOW CONTINUES

It was the third season that Gregg and Tommy would play together. It really did not matter who they played against. They always made the opposition look like school kids trying to cover the two speedsters. Katie, Jon, and Jessie sat together for the games. They were matched up against Minnesota in the twin cities. Gregg and Tommy had arranged for the whole of the Carlton Bulldogs to be at the game. Herman was now a Senior and starting quarterback for the Bulldogs. He wanted to watch the pro quarterbacks see if he could pick up any tips from the team. Kevin Derusha was hoping to watch some linebackers do crunch jobs on running backs. He also wanted to watch them in pass coverage to see what points he could pick up there. Both young men knew that they had one year left to play high school ball. They also understood from talking to college and pro players that the most fun any of the players had was playing high school ball. They did not realize yet that God the Father was watching them and had plans to introduce them to himself in some real ways on the football team.

_ * _

"Pete, watch what I do with these school kids. I will give them a season that will knock their socks off if they are willing to put the work into it needed to accomplish all they can with the gifts that I have given them. They will have so much fun, and the rewards that every young man on the team receives will be never-ending. But Pete, they won't be the only ones having fun." The Father of all mankind said as he chuckled.

_ * _

Herman's last year at Carlton would be pure magic. The Father would be watching in tandem with the Son and the Holy Spirit as Herman, and the gang would guide Carlton to Its first state championship in football. Which would set him up to be recruited by Minnesota State. Tommy, on the other hand, was looking at his career. He looked up to heaven. "Father, one year, I just want one year to be able to play pro-ball with Herman McBrien. You set up that day in that restaurant years back that you would use Jill McBrien to give me life. Then later, you would use her again to give life to Herman. Father, my deepest desire is to have us 'brothers' play one year, just one year together?"

_ * _

The Father was smiling ear to ear. "Pete, when Herman and Tommy play together, every game is going to be electric. When Herman realizes all they must do to complete a pass is get it close to Tommy, the wins they will be able to achieve are going to break TNFC records for the next hundred years; just watch."

_ * _

Herman signed a letter of intent with Minnesota. He would spend his collegiate years in the frozen tundra of Minnesota. In the meantime, Tommy would become more and more dominant as a wide receiver for Dallas. But deep down, he wanted just one year playing with Herman. They would talk on the phone till late at night. Tommy could get across what to look for in separation to know if a man were open, or the cornerback could disguise the coverage enough to set a trap that the quarterback would throw into. Coming at it from the wide receiver angle, Tommy could share some insights and discuss signals that a receiver could quickly flash at the quarterback to let him know not to throw to him.

Tommy and Gregg would be a masterful team. The opposition would become more and more intimidated by them. The Sunday they played New York was no different. The game was a slugfest on the line of scrimmage. Yet the two receivers would blow open the defenses. The final score was 53 to 30 Dallas.

13. THE LAST SEASON

The next three years would go by quickly. The duo of Richardson and Shoemaker would tear up the football fields both at home and in other cities, where they were the visiting teams. Two Superbowl rings in two years would put smiles on everyone's face. Yet in the back of Tommy's mind was the dream of catching touchdown passes from Herman McBrien. Herman's senior year would see him win the most coveted award a college football player could win. The Heisman award. Tommy had a light go on inside of his head. He went to the front office for Dallas and asked them if they would look at Tommy in the draft. He explained to them again the relationship between the two of them and that his dream was to play his last season with Herman. Joe Smith, the owner, looked at Tommy, a loyal player who always gave everything he had for the team. He realized that this was about more than just football. He realized that deep down, there was a connection that if they made it possible one way or the other for Tommy to play his last season with Herman, the memories he had for Dallas would be something sweet that would be passed on to other players for generations to come.

Draft day came. In desperate need of a quarterback, Minnesota drafted their hometown boy in the first round. That left Tommy wondering if his dream, ever since childhood, would go the way of the dinosaurs. He thought it was something that would be lost forever. Joe Smith called Tommy into his office.

Joe had the original contract that Tommy had signed 8 years previous. "Mr. Richardson, as I look at this contract, I see we have a bit of a problem," Joe said, smiling. "It appears we have a subparagraph that if Herman McBrien ever makes the pros, either we will draft him or try to trade you to the team that signs him. I am now aware we could not sign him; he was chosen by Minnesota. I also understand that next season will be your last in the league. To be honest, we do not want to see you go. We would love to have you play your last season with us. We are willing to give you a sizable bonus to stay your last year here. But I am willing to let you go if that's what you need to see your career complete." Joe said.

Tommy had a pit in his stomach. His dream throughout his career had been to play his last year with Herman. He knew that this decision, if he chose wrong, would haunt him for the rest of his life. He took one long look at the numbers that had been put in front of him. His agent, Tom Livingston, looked at the figures and was about to say they would take it. Tommy spoke up. "Trade me." Tom bit his tongue. A tear started to come to his eye. He could see his percentage slipping away. But he knew this meant a lot to Tommy and did not try to change his mind.

Then Joe had an idea to try to trade and get Herman. He called the owner of Minnesota and found out rather quickly that that would not happen. So, he proceeded to see who he would be willing to trade for Tommy. "Tommy Richardson, why would you want to trade him?" the Owner of Minnesota asked.

For the next ½ hour, Joe would explain the original contract and that Tommy's dream has always been to play football with Herman McBrien. "What are you looking to get for Tommy. You know as well as I do this could be his last year. But having him with Herman might just get us that Superbowl win that has been so elusive over all of these years."

A light went on inside of Joe's head. "How about your first-round draft pick next year, and you are third the year after. Putting Herman and Tommy together for one year with you guys could be real magic." Joe said.

"That, my friend, maybe workable. That way, everyone gets what they want out of this thing. Why don't I fly down next week, and we really put this thing together?" Minnesota's owner said.

Joe picked up the phone. "Tommy, as much as I hate to see you go, I think we have been able to hammer out a deal. Next winter, you will be freezing your behind-off in Minnesota. I wish you the best with them unless you are playing us." Joe said laughing."

"Big Joe, I will never be able to show my gratitude for this. But know this, You will be remembered as a man of your word."

14. THEY MEET IN MINNESOTA, AGAIN!

It was the first day of practice. Tommy walked into the locker room and was sitting there when rookie Herman McBrien walked in. Herman was not expecting to see Tommy sitting there when he walked in. Herman's jaw dropped and just about hit the floor. The expression on his face was priceless as he looked over at one of the greatest wide receivers that had ever played football. "Are you going to be playing with Minnesota this year?" He stammered.

Tommy smiled. "Hermey, it's been my dream to have you throwing touchdown passes to me. One thing we must keep in mind is this. Christ is always first in everything we do. We honor him both on the field and off. As we do that, the victories are going to come. Tommy, this is going to be my last season. Let's make it a great one. I think they probably drafted you to start this season. That's not the way franchises usually do it, but Jeb Frank had a career-ending injury last season, and they needed someone who could step in and be adequate. You work hard with me this season, and people will see our Father's greatness through His Son Jesus by His Holy Spirit has built into you. After we get done together, you will throw too many great receivers. Some will be better than I am. I know that. There is always someone better. But know this, what you will learn by playing football with me is this. Keep your priorities focused on the big prize, that Christ and his kingdom. Even if we win the Super Bowl, in the big scheme of things, it means very little, if because of the position he has placed you in, you can be an example to young people what it means to be a Christian, and that draws them to a saving knowledge, then you have accomplished something."

Herman looked directly into Tommy's eyes. "Tommy, I feel like I have been close to you for years, even though we have not even been in the same locality. Our connection through my mom is like we both owe our lives to her. I guess we do in a sense; that makes us brothers. We do have to keep this whole thing in perspective. We both know why we have been given the talent to be playing football. That is to draw young men and women to Christ. To see lives and change at an early stage to change other young people forever. That means a couple of things. Number 1. We must always play at the top of our game; number 2 is to live our lives so that being a Christ-follower becomes attractive to the young people because of the life we are living. We do have our work cut out for us. My brother, this is going to be a fun year." Tommy said.

With that, Herman picked up a football and said. "Go deep." Tommy sprinted about 65 yards down the field, and Herman hit him right in the palms of his hands. Tommy jogged back. Smiled at Herman and stated robustly.

"This is going to be a fun year."

The two of them looked at the schedule. It would be a brutal year. They realized that the schedule had them playing both teams in last year's super bowl. Which meant that they would be playing Dallas. This also meant that Tommy would be playing against the cornerback that he had to practice against every day for 8 years. Tommy looked at Herman, "Like I said, this will be a fun season."

The Dallas game would prove challenging. They would have Tommy covered like a blanket, but Phil Smith would prove to be the diamond in the rough in this game. Herman would find him time and again. Tommy would be wide open when they would slide coverage over onto Phil. The same thing they had accomplished for years with Gregg and Tommy was now being done to them with Phil and Tommy. Herman loved having receivers that would catch any ball that Herman could get close to them. Normally the passes were all right on the money but being a rookie and starting in the league came with a price. He was blessed to have a couple of top-notch wide receivers and a couple of backs who could grab anything in the proximity of where they were at. On one play, Herman was being rushed by Jake Thompson, who could always break free and slam quarterbacks. He had put three out of commission last year. In this play, he had a bead on Herman that had Hermie running for his life. Herman spotted Floyd Merriweather running free in the secondary. He got the ball in his vicinity, hoping for an incompletion that would stop the rush. Merriweather caught the ball in stride, had a 40-yard gain, and was spotted on the two-yard line. Two plays later, Herman rewarded him by hitting him with a perfect short pass for a touchdown. Herman would throw two more touchdowns that game. One to Tommy and one more to Phil Smith as he streaked down the sideline for an 80-yard touchdown. Things were looking bright for the season as this was only their second game.

_ * _

The Father looked over at Peter." Pete, now do you understand why I started this whole thing back when Eli and Jill went out to breakfast at that nice restaurant on the beach. Do you understand why knowing that Jill had the same blood type as Tommy would be important? You see, I was looking at the thousands of young people Tommy would reach through the years. I knew the raw talent I had instilled in Tommy. I knew that the relationship between Tommy and Herman would be that of brothers. Both brothers in a personal relationship, and brothers in me. You see, the blood I had flowed through Jill's veins would always be flowing through the brothers. Through this, Jill and Janet, Tommy's mom, would become lifelong friends. I have a way of building friendships that will never end.

Peter looked at the Father who created the love that saved all mankind who would accept it in his Son Jesus. He also knew that the faith of millions of young men and women would be ignited because of the love gained by that breakfast years before.

_ * _

As they walked out of the locker room after defeating Dallas, the crowd was enormous, waiting for them. Suddenly he heard a voice he had not heard in a while. "Tommy, Tommy Richardson!" Tommy looked around. He spotted two women standing next to each other. One was Jill McBrien, the other his mom Janet.

Jill and Eli were standing next to Janet. "We would like to invite you two great players out to eat tonight. We are going back to the same place where we met in honor. The place on the beach. Shall we go?" Eli said with a smile on his face.

Tommy looked at Herman and his wife Katie, who had just arrived. Feeling like little boys who had just played their first game, both men smiled at the same time. "You know what, When I was a kid and would have a great game, we used to go to a place called Lipinski's Dairy Queen. What do you say we hit the nearest DQ as a celebration of that time together?"

In unison, the group let out a huge yell. "Let's do it!" Eli walked with his beautiful bride Jill back to their rental for the weekend. "A Dodge Challenger with a Hemi. This car brought back memories of his first date with Jill. As they rode around in it, they were almost giddy with the memories that they were having. Jill looked at Eli with her penetrating blue eyes that Eli loved as much now as the time of their first date. "Babes, I will never forget that night. I brought you home, and your dad sent you into the house. He made me make that promise that even today makes me tremble a little bit. I wondered as I drove off, squealing those tires on that Challenger that my Dad had bought me. How could I ever keep that promise with such a hot girlfriend? But you know what, I think I had a little angel sitting on my shoulder. Every time I would even think of breaking that promise, it was like that little angel was speaking in my ear. Yup, and I wonder what God the Father, through His Son Jesus by His Holy Spirit, had named him?

_ * _

The Thumbnail celebrating the results of what the Father has placed him with them to do was giddy. "It was me! It was Me!" He was shouting. Eli looked around the car, wondering what he was hearing. But then he just wrote it off.

The Father looked at his littlest angel and decided to let him bask in the glory of the moment. He could see he was having a whole lot of fun and did not want to dispel that even for a second. "Thumbnail, I am so proud of what you did following my instructions with this young couple. We worked together and followed the instructions that I had you pass on to them. You proved yourself to be a good and faithful servant. Well done, little one!"

— * —

At that second, Herman walked up to his parents. "What are you folks discussing?" He asked.

"Herman, It was before you were born. We had just lost your little sister and had gone out to breakfast. That's when the Lord put us together with Tommy and his mom. That was the day you would become the brother of Tommy Richardson. That was the day when his world would change and change yours before you were even born." Eli answered.

"I'll tell ya, dad, I have never been able to throw to anyone like Tommy. All I do is get the ball close to him, and it's a catch. This is going to be one great year. It's just too bad it's at the end of his career. But we will have a fun year." Herman said with great excitement and just a touch of disappointment in his voice.

Their second game of the season was against Phoenix. Herman saw Tommy, who appeared to be wide open. The coverage was well disguised. Tommy caught the pass and was laid out so hard by the Phoenix defender Tommy thought he may have broken his jaw. He did not, but the hit was brutal. On the next play, they would get within field goal range and be stopped. Smith, their field goal kicker, easily put the ball through the uprights for 3 points. On the sidelines, Tommy pulled Herman aside. "Herm, you have got to watch that a little better. The guys at this level have a way of disguising their coverages. Unless you see what's going on, you will leave your receivers open for some brutal hits. None of which will make your receivers happy about getting laid out after the catch. They may catch them, but they will pay a dear price for catching that ball. Believe me, I know that last hit was brutal, and those corners were more than willing to let a receiver have it and hard."

Herman nodded. "Tommy, I did not even see the defender close to you. If I had, I would have placed the ball in a better situation for you. Never in high school or at the U. did I have people who could disguise coverage that well. Let's talk to coach Johansson and see if there is some way I can see those coverages better.

Tommy smiled. "Hermie, I have seen a lot of things in this league. As soon as I made the cut, I knew I was not open. I could almost feel him, He was close, and I knew you could not see it. I knew I would pay for that catch. Let's take him out next time, and we will make him pay for it. Let me run a couple of decoys and see where he is at. I will tell you what pattern to call." Tommy said, smiling.

Herman had Tommy set up as a decoy to feel out where Scott Smith would be playing when Tommy made his cut in the next play. Herman purposely threw the ball away. But he had the info he needed. Tommy walked into the huddle, looked at Herman, and winked. "27 fades cut right deep." Hermie then called that exact play. He knew where Tommy would be before he threw the ball. He dropped back and just threw the ball where Tommy would be. Tommy would catch it and run untouched 45 yards into the endzone. The crowd went wild.

Minnesota would beat Phoenix 23 to 17 for their second victory of the season. As they walked into the locker room, the place was bedlam. Guys were screaming and totally enjoying their victory. After the game, Herman and Tommy and Eli and Jill and Tommy's wife Abby all went out to eat in the nicest place in town. Janet sat with Tommy, Abby, and Eli, and Jill sat next to them. Tommy looked at Eli and said. "Eli, you have raised a great young man there. I am surprised he is not going to play baseball, but he could hit a dime at fifty yards, quarterbacks like him are a receiver's dream." Tommy said. Then he looked at Jill. "Jill, how can I thank you for giving me life. Without you, I would be watching all of this beside Jesus and St. Peter in heaven. It shows what those little nudges can lead to." He got up, walked over to her table, and asked. "Jill McBrien, could I give you a hug?"

Jill smiled at him as she stood up. "You know it, young man. But know this. Through His Son by His Spirit, God the Father gave you time on this earth for a reason. Besides catching a football, you better start praying, young man, for the Father to lead you into the ministry he has for you. You may want to look at coaching at a level where the kids are most vulnerable, and you would be able to make a difference in their life." Then she threw her arms around his neck and gave her first son by transplant a hug he would never forget. After the hug Tommy looked at his other "mom." "I think you are right; there is life after football. For years I have been a hero to young people. I have given of myself to establish ministries wherever the lord put me. In Dallas, I worked with some other players to establish the Jesus Center for kids in downtown Dallas.

Now it is time to really get things in gear. I have an idea that might work after the season is over. When I walk off the field for the last time. When I feel that sense of "it's over." I do not know exactly what it will look like, but I know. Football has been my life. Yet there is more. I know God the Father through His Son by His Spirit has put me in this position to see lives changed forever. He went through a lot of trouble back in LA. To put us together. It's now time to be used to touching kids. To show that there is life after playing football. Football is a picture of life. It shows the greatness that can be established when guys come together with a common goal. Great things can be accomplished when that goal is reaching people for Christ through the sport. You will start to see lives changed forever."

15. THAT FINAL SEASON

Team after team would fall to Minnesota that year. They were amazing all the sports writers. They did not want to see the season end, but both Herman and Tommy realized that with each game, the dream they were living out was coming to a time when they would wake up. They both realized that Tommy was ending his pro career with the one brother to him, Herman. Tommy realized that his quickness was not what it was even four years ago.

Sunday, October 15th, they would be in Seattle. They realized that they were coming into a time halfway through their season together when they were about to prove just how great a combination Minnesota had for the year. They were sitting in the locker room, getting ready for the game. Tommy said, "that number 29, Johnson is really quick; I am going to have to do some hard work to beat this guy; I think if you run the 36 spring right throwback, we can take this guy out."

Herman smiled as he stated, you run the route; the ball will be there where you need it. Let's have some fun with this guy."

Tommy just smiled as the coach walked by. "What are you guys discussing?" he asked.

Herman looked at the coach. "We were discussing running 36 spring throwback against number 29. I think we can take him out with that." Herman said.

The coach smiled. "Herman, you have got a real handle on our offense. I will let you know when the time is right to bust this game open with the play."

The game would prove to be brutal. Some of Tommy's hits were making him wish that he had retired last year. All he knew was that every game won got them closer to their goal. The score was tied at 3 apiece. Midway through the second quarter, the play came in from the sidelines. 36 spring throwback. Herman and Tommy smiled at each other. They knew they had that guy. And boy, were they right.

Herman walked behind his center Thornton. He smiled as he looked over the defense. Barked out the signals, took the snap, and sprinted to his right. Tommy was streaking down the left with what looked like a fly pattern. Johnson was running stride for stride with him. Tommy hit the brakes, and Johnson ran right by him, caught Herman's pass, sprinted to this right a few yards, then hit the endzone for an easy touchdown. The crowd went totally nuts. The screams and moans as the hometown fans realized that Minnesota had just started what would turn into a blowout. The exuberance injected into Minnesota would carry them through the rest of the game and to a victory.

The brotherhood that would be built between them this one season would carry them through the rest of their lives. But their mutual passion would eventually lead them to be in a situation that would surprise everyone. As the season went on, the question that went on through both of their minds at the beginning of their pro careers would be answered. "What does all this mean in the big scheme of things?" Their Father in Heaven would show them what it all meant. He would show them how a football game could teach young men what working together as a team for a common goal would do for the whole organization.

Their next game would be against Green Bay. As Herman walked into the locker room on Monday, there was a whole new atmosphere. His mind went back to Carlton when they played Esko. The hatred the two teams had for each other was obvious. No matter how good they were, Carlton seemed to always get beat by the Eskimos. As he thought about Green Bay, he could not help but think about the past games against Esko. His mind would go over and over those games. Suddenly his coach popped him out of his bubble. "McBrien, get your head in the game. I don't know what's going on but fix it." He said in a very intense voice and walked away.

Tommy walked up to Herman and put his arm around his shoulder. "Hermey: it's time to get the high school psyche out of your mind. I have received some of the passes that you should not have been able to get to me. At this stage in the game, you can be one of the greatest ever to step on the field. The question is this. How bad do you want it? You are thinking to how you may have blown a game that you really needed to win against Esko in the back of your mind. Get that game out of your head. You're a professional now. Act and play like it." With that, Tommy walked away and left Herman standing in his own shadow.

That night Herman lay in his bed in his beautiful new home. He got up and walked around seeking the Face of God the Father through His Son Jesus by His Holy Spirit. "Father, your word says that perfect love casts out all fear. Your word tells us over and over to fear not. Over the years, I have seen you do some amazing things with me getting the ball to the right receiver at the right place and at the right time. Why does this game scare me so much with Green Bay? What are you trying to show me about myself?"

Thumbnail was sitting on his shoulder. "Herman, you need to give this game to the Father. You need to trust that His Son Jesus paid the price for your sin, and if you give anything that comes against you, give it over to the Father through Jesus by His Spirit; he will lead you into victories that, as he said about your dad will astound people. It's time for you to surrender to the Lordship of Christ. As you do this, and you work your butt off, you will see victories of the Father through the Son by the Spirit in all aspects of your life. The time for going for it is now. It's time to go to work and go get the victories that the Father through the Son by the Spirit has created you for." Then Thumbnail made his way back to the Father.

Herman had heard Thumbnail loud and clear. He just had no clue who had been talking to him. He did not recognize the higher pitch of the voice. Besides that, he could not see who was talking to him. All he knew was that he really wanted to play in a way that pleased the Father through the Son by the Spirit. He started to understand that fear had no part in what The Father would do. All he knew was that he had to be an obedient servant to the Holy Trinity. He understood the rest of the team had put their trust in him. He also knew that the team was investing a huge sum of money in his salary, and he wanted to know that he was earning it. There was only one way to do that. That was to keep throwing touchdown passes to Tommy Richardson this year. He walked up to Tommy. "Tommy, if you can get open against Ripken, you will have the ball laid in your hands like a baby. The only thing between you and the endzone will be sunlight and air.

Tommy smiled at Herman. "Bro, let's get by these guys and keep moving onto the show. We have only this season together; we must make the most of it. We cannot let up even for one game. You see, winners in the league have multiple venues open to them when they retire. As for me, next year, I will be coaching varsity football back at Carlton High School. I know this; next year, those kids will work their butts off. But they will know that the Father in heaven has a place for them in his plan."

Herman smiled and walked over and shook Tommy's hand. "Bro let's make this happen; I know you are stretching out your career by one year so we can play together. That shows me the love of a brother. There are few loves stronger than the love between brothers. I love you, bro!" He stated with a smile.

16. THE SEASON GETS TOUGH

The Father looked over at Peter. "Pete: You're about to see what happens when two men become brothers through the selfless act of one woman. These two men are going to start something that will go on long after I bring them both home. Sometimes it takes years for the fruits of my creation to come to where they are supposed to be. But, if the two brothers keep their eyes on me, they can accomplish great things through me. They will accomplish some great things this year on the football field. But the real greatness will start next year.

Tuesday night, after practice, Tommy and Herman walked out of the stadium. Both had a smile on their face as they headed to their respective cars. Tommy looked at Herman and said. "Herman, that new pass pattern the coach installed is going to be very productive, I think; both cornerbacks, Hansen, and Corker could not even come close to covering it. They are two of the best, not even close. This is going to be fun."

"I know, as long as I have time to get the ball to you, we will be fine. I don't even know why I would say that bro, I have not had any trouble sitting back there for as long I needed to to get the ball to you. This is going to be fun."

Sunday would come around quickly. Their opponent was Chicago. Even in their down years, they were a force to be reckoned with. This Sunday would be no different. Herman would find himself getting "sacked" three times but still could complete 25 passes for 3 touchdowns. He was to find Tommy in the endzone for two of them. As the team went into the locker room after the game, the hooting and hollering were deafening. Herman's mind went back to his senior year of Highschool went they beat the infamous Esko Eskomos. The volume was not even that high in the Minnesota locker room. But Herman relished that same feeling of exuberance. The ride to the airport on the team bus was totally emotional. The players were like a bunch of high school players. Until the coach got up in front of the bus. "Guys, I don't want to throw too much cold water on your celebration but remember, next weekend we have Miami. Enjoy this victory, but keep in mind how sweet it will be to take out Miami. I want you to go over the plays in your sleep. When crunch time comes one week from today, you better be ready."

The next week at practice would be tough. The defense was getting ready for the speedsters in the receiving corps of Miami. They knew that they had to be ready. Tommy was doing his best to beat his own D-back. He knew that if they could cover him, they would be able to cover just about anybody that Miami could throw at them.

Sunday, October 15. Miami stadium. As Tommy and Herman walked out on the stadium floor and looked up into the stands, they could not help but smile. "Herman, I feel a little bad. We are going to have a good part of the Miami fans leaving this stadium disappointed, their team will lose today, and if we have anything to say about it, they will lose big.

The game was brutal. Herman dropped back and spotted Tommy wide open in the endzone. He threw the ball and was leveled by Gerry Thompson. He laid on the ground watching the birdies soar around his head, or so he thought. With the touchdown, the crowd went silent. He laid there looking up and the sun shining on the field. He moved both feet than his arms, making sure all was still workable. Throughout his years in high school and college, he had never been hit that hard. Thompson walked up to him, offered Herman his hand, and helped him up. "Welcome to the pros. McBrien. Get used to getting hit like that; you will get many more." Then he turned and walked away.

Herman made his way to the sidelines. He looked to the stands and saw an old teammate of his. Kevin Derusha. He waved and called the ball boy over; he pointed to Derusha and sent a note to meet him after the game. Herman would stay away from Thompson the rest of the game. On the sidelines, he called a huddle with all his line men over. "Hey guys, this is a team sport; Thompson about crushed me on that play. Please do what you can to keep him off my ass. We all make more money when we win. Let's see if we can win this one. You keep the defense off me, dinners on me tonight." He said with a wink and a smile.

In the Locker room they tried to give Tommy the game ball. He then tried to give it to Herman, who called the whole offensive line and handed them the game ball. For the rest of the game, no one even got close to Herman, they were even able to run and end around, and Tommy would run 96 yards for a touchdown. Tommy smiled as he said, "These guys earned it. One little hiccup in the 1st quarter, and after that, no one got close to us. You can have the best backs in the world; they are worthless without a great line. And we do have a great line."

The line men were strutting their stuff. They knew they had done an amazing job that day. The coach looked at them and smiled ear to ear. Now he had a team. Dinner that night was amazing for the line.

October 23rd

The team would find themselves in Cincinnati, Ohio. They were to play Cincinnati in what would prove to be the game that would really test their metal. Herman dropped back to pass on the first play and got wiped out by Quasi-moto. The big china man was imported from Hong Kong. Herman walked into the huddle and looked at his linemen with "the look." They knew he was not happy with the last play. That was all it took; they would not get anywhere near him for the rest of the game. Three touchdown passes were all it took. Herman threw two to Tommy and one to Ripken. Then for good measure, Jon Smith intercepted a pass from Jockular Kabul and returned it for another touchdown. Final score: Minnesota 36 Cincinnati 14.

Halloween October 31st. Minnesota was in Frisco. The 39rs thought they would be able to put a stop to Minnesota's perfect season.

On the flight out, Herman was sitting with Tommy. Herman looked at Tommy and asked a question. "Why not perfect. Only one other team has accomplished; why not us?"

Herman about coughed on his sandwich. "You do realize I am a rookie, do you not?" Herman asked.

"What can't God do?" Tommy answered. Remember Jesus was the one who said, "All things are possible if you only believe." "By the way, the reference is Mark 9:23. You see, my brother, if we believe that is what God is calling us to, and we work our butts off to accomplish it, then it's his responsibility to make it happen."

Herman stood up to stretch his legs. "I am willing to put in the work. I am willing to do my part. God shows up; this could be an exciting rest of the season."

Frisco was the Gay capital of the world. As they walked into the stands, one could sense something evil in the air. The team gathered around Tommy in the huddle on the 50-yard line. They prayed that God the Father, through His Son Jesus by His Holy Spirit, would put the enemy to shame that night. They prayed for such a huge victory that after the Game, Herman and Tommy would be able to tell the reporters why they would be playing with a vengeance that night.

Frisco would come out with guns blazing. The problem was they got stuffed before they could get off the line of scrimmage. That night Herman would hit Tommy with 4 touchdown passes and run for one more. Frisco would manage to score one touchdown and a field goal. A big linebacker trying to blitz Herman all night after the game, John Smith, walked up to Herman. "What is it you guys have. We were not able to get even close to you tonight?" He asked.

Herman smile at John. "John, it's like this. I have Jesus leading every part of my life. It is evil in this town. We prayed in the huddle that the Holy Spirit would destroy the works of the evil one. That a mark would be made that we would be used to destroy what the enemy was trying to do in this town."

Smith smiled. "I am a believer as well. I was drafted to come here to play. But to be honest, I feel it every day I am here. When you talk to the press, make that same point to them." He replied.

In the locker room, the press was there. Harry Junkyard asked Herman a question. "You guys played amazingly well tonight. To what do you attribute the performance tonight?" He asked Herman.

Herman looked at his coach, knowing what he wanted to say and knowing his coach knew what he wanted to say as well. His coach nodded. "Harry, it's like this. You saw us huddle on the 50-yard line right before the national anthem. We prayed that we would be used to, in part, have a hand in defeating the evil that has taken over this city. We had an energy that we have never felt before going into a game."

Harry got a look of confusion on his face. "And what would that evil be?" He asked.

The look on Herman's face got serious. "I am going to be blunt. My degree is in biology with an emphasis on pre-med. For homosexuality to survive, it must always get new blood. It cannot reproduce any other way. A person's first sexual experience will leave an impression that will last a lifetime. Most young boys overcame it, but then some could not. The scar lasts for life. That must stop. God created Adam and Eve. Not Adam and Steve.

Herman and Tommy could see Harry biting his lower lip. Being gay, he did not want to let out what happened to him as a young boy. The anger at what had happened to him was building inside of him for a long time. He just did not want to deal with these two-football heroes on the topic. He could see that Herman and Tommy were well-educated men and that taking them on would only hurt his credibility. "You do realize that in this town if I put in print what you just told me, they will want to hang you out to dry, don't you?"

Tommy stepped up to the mic. He looked over the crowd of reporters. "Harry, you do realize that there are going to be a bunch of guys printing and broadcasting what we said, don't you?"

Harry stood up. "Can I talk to you guys privately when we finish here? Our conversation will be off the record. There is something in my life I need to deal with?"

"We would, but we have to catch a flight as soon as we are done here," Tommy said.

"Then I will fly to Minnesota tomorrow," Harry answered.
Tommy smiled. "Works for us."
The flight back was getting late; both Tommy and Herman could sleep as the team plane flew from Frisco the Minneapolis. Both

hopped in the cars, kept in a separate hanger for the team and coaches. And went home to get some sleep.

Monday Tommy was going to take the day off with his bride. He walked down into the kitchen, and his phone went off. "Tommy, Harry here. Can I buy your breakfast?"

Tommy smiled, looked at his bride Kate, and she nodded. "Sure, let's meet at Marks downtown?"

Two hours later, the two men met for breakfast. Marks was an old-fashioned breakfast spot. Nothing fancy, just great food. Harry looked across the table at Tommy. "You know that young man you talked about and his first sexual experience being what would mark him for life?" He asked.

"Yes," Tommy answered.

"That young man was me," Harry said.

Tommy sat back in his chair. "I am sorry," Tommy said.

"Nothing to be sorry about. I am who I am." Harry answered.

Tommy straightened himself. "You are not who God the Father through His Son by His Spirit created you to be. If you surrender to Christ, He can change you from the inside out; if you want to be clean, he will cleanse you."

"Mr. Richardson, we in the gay community know what we are doing is wrong. We know that it was not God who made us "gay." We think we are in love, but we really don't know what love is. My problem is I don't know how to get out." Harry stated.

Tommy looked Harry directly in the eyes. "You start with prayer and with surrender to Christ. Are you willing to do that?" He asked.

Harry nodded. "I think that would be a good start." With that, Tommy led Harry in a prayer of commitment to Christ. Then Harry looked at Tommy. "I think I need to move away from Frisco. It's like God is talking to me big time."

Tommy pulled out his pocket testament. Turned to 1st Corinthians 15:33. Handed it to Harry and asked him to read it out loud. "Bad Company is the ruin of good morals. Yup, I guess it's what God really does want me to do. He wants me to keep focused on his plan, not my own. I think my name is well enough known that I could become a freelance writer and, by doing so, could reach a great many people with the message. What do you think?" Harry asked Tommy.

Tommy smiled. "Harry, you are extremely talented playing football. You hit me so hard yesterday when I caught that first pass from Herman, I did not think I would ever get up. But this is the crux of the situation; if you get out of Frisco, you need to get traded or retire. You have a few good years left in you; you could make a few more million dollars. Doing so would place you in a great situation to accomplish some great things. You will have kids looking up to you in a way that will give them excitement for the game. You will be able to speak into their lives in a way that could make a huge difference in their future. I think this is something we really need to be in prayer about."

"I hear what you are saying, Tommy. I will be asking for a trade at the end of this season. That means I really need to keep my focus on accomplishing God's greatness on the field. He will then use that greatness to touch kids and adults, for that matter, off the field." Harry said.

The three-star players said their goodbyes and headed in opposite directions. As Tommy and Herman walked down the walkway, Herman turned to Tommy and said. "Tommy, I thank God that he has me throwing to you. I realize that we have a limited amount of time left to play together. Let's make the most of it, bro, and take home that one prize every player in football wants. The Superbowl. "

Tommy gave a little chuckle. "Bro, I just want your mom to be proud of what the two men she gave life to when they are totally focused on Christ and His kingdom can accomplish. If it were not for your mom, neither would we be here. I am just thankful that our Father in heaven has chosen us to carry his message. Tomorrow, when we get back to the twin cities, I have some time with the Boys and Girls club. Are you with me?"

Herman nodded. "How can I not be with you. We have been given these roles playing a kid's game and making millions of dollars for one reason. That is to reach kids. You bet I will go with you tomorrow." Herman said, smiling.

- * -

The Father of all mankind looked at his servant Peter and smiled. "Pete, I love doing stuff like this. When my kids get it, I mean, really get it; my excitement is like a kid waking up on Christmas morning with excitement that just cannot be squelched. To see my kids who have worked hard to accomplish the greatness that I built into them, take that greatness and pour it into other kids of mine so they can become who I have created them to be. Nothing better. When my kids work hard, I reward their efforts." The Father of all mankind said.

_ * _

As Herman and Tommy drove up to the "club," the kids ran out with an excitement that could not be contained. Most of whom were coming from less than stellar homes, these kids were excited to meet "famous" football players. Tommy smiled at them warmly and started to speak. "Kids, relax. We are here to help you figure out what path the Father of all mankind has set for you through His Son Jesus by His Holy Spirit. Remember this. If you are willing to work hard the gifts, he has given you will be multiplied, and your greatness is only hindered by you. If you are willing to let the Father work through you, you will be amazed by what you can accomplish."

They would spend the next several hours just listening to the kids' talking about what they felt they could become. Some children in middle school were speaking about accomplishing some great things in sports. Others wanted to go into medicine or even into space exploration. One young man wanted to become a submarine in the Navy. What Tommy and Herman found themselves asking each of the young people at the boy's and girl's club was just how hard they were willing to work to accomplish what the giftings the Father had given them.

Tommy stood up in front of the kids and asked them a question. "How much work do you think it took for me to become the receiver that I am today or the quarterback that Herman has become?"

Kevin Johnson spoke up. "Lots. I mean a whole bunch. You don't learn the skills that you have overnight."

Herman chuckled a bit. "Well, Kevin, it's like this. I found my passion for throwing a football at Elim Lutheran Church back in the day. Some of my buddies had me throw passes to them. It got a bit tricky at times. I needed coaching to help me become all that The Father through His Son Jesus by His Spirit wanted and created me to be. I don't even know if I am at the level now that he really wants me, but I have to keep working to improve my throwing, reading of defenses, and playing calling to be the best at what the Father has created me to be. That's where he has all of us. We must keep improving at what he has called us to do. The Holy Spirit will enable us to accomplish great things with what he has given us. We just must be willing to give at least 100 percent all the time. He has created greatness in all of us. But we must pour ourselves into our gifts all day, every day to accomplish what God the Father created us for."

At that point, John Jacobson walked into the meeting room." Gentlemen, I am afraid it's closing time. I have parents waiting in cars outside, wondering what is taking them so long. Would you gentlemen walk out with the youngsters and share with the parents what you discussed with the Children what you talked about?"

As Tommy and Herman walked out, they looked at some parents who had been waiting over an hour as the meeting with the young people ran way over. The parents started to get out of their cars as they walked out. John Edwards, one of the dads, got out of his car. He was a huge football fan and loved Minnesota. He saw Tommy and ran up to him. "Mr. Richardson, I am a huge fan. Could I get your autograph?"

Tommy Chuckled. "You bet you can!" John pulled out a notebook he had sitting in his car and handed it to Tommy.

" John, I just spent an hour working with your son Chad. You should be proud of that young man. He wants to follow in your footsteps and go into medicine. Do whatever it takes to help him accomplish what he has been created by our Father in Heaven to accomplish. Our Father in heaven gives the gifts. It's our responsibility to accomplish as much as we can with the gifts we have been given." That is what he wrote to Chad's dad.

John read what was written by Tommy. As Tommy shook John's hand, he looked him in the eye and said. "John, you have a much more important job than I do right now. I entertain people; you save their lives."

John looked back at Tommy. "Mr. Richardson, do you realize that by taking the time to invest in these young people, you are saving their lives as well. You see, God has given you the ability to catch a football. That gets the attention of the young people and allows you to be able to speak into their lives. Without being the player, you are, those doors would not have been open. You would be just another Joe Blow on

Tommy

the street. Football is the Father's platform that has given you these last 12 years to accomplish greatness that would allow you to speak into these kids' lives now. Remember, Tommy, some of these kids were not born yet when you started playing. They have grown up with you being a household name. The Father has placed you in this position for a reason. He wants to touch kids through you. He wants to draw kids into his presence by using you. I can't do that; in most cases, in what I do, you can do it every day. Believe me, I am going to watch you go through the playoffs. My son and I will be in our box seats watching you win that trip to the Superbowl."

With three games left in the regular season, neither Herman nor Tommy wanted to look beyond them to the playoffs. Minnesota had Detroit breathing down their neck, and neither player could afford a distraction. Tuesday, the first practice getting ready for Philadelphia, they worked especially hard. The two of them would spend the time going over the playbook after practice. They needed to make sure that every pass, and the trick plays, if they used them, would go off as planned.

_ * _

The Father looked at St. Pete. "Peter, I put my plays into the minds of men. It does not matter if those plays are on a football field, a basketball court, baseball diamond, or even in a courtroom; I can see what the enemy of men's souls is trying to do to my kids. If they are trying to take away freedoms that I have enshrined in my word and their country's constitution, I make sure my kids have the plays to get the victory. If they are willing to put in the work, I will give my kids victories that will and do astound people. Herman and Tommy are putting in hours and hours getting the plays down to be used against Philly. I am going to bless those plays when the time comes to pull the trigger with them." The Father said.

_ * _

Tommy and Herman would repeatedly run Hutch's 49 counter pass as they worked to be ready for Sunday's game against Philadelphia. Over and over again, the pass would fall into Herman's hand from Tommy's perfect pass. After Friday's practice, they would spend time with Joe Smith and Johnson praying about the game that would be coming up. As they walked out of the practice facility Abby Jenson, the cutest reporter in town, walked up to Herman to ask him a couple of questions. "Mr. McBrien, you were and are a great quarterback. May I ask you some questions."

Herman looked over all the standing press, trying to get his attention. He pointed to Abby and motioned for her to come close. When she walked up to him and quietly put a proposition forth. "Abby, I will give you one-on-one over dinner. That's the best I can do. Justin's by the beach, ok? "

Abby stepped back. "Mr. McBrien, are you propositioning me?"

Abby, if you know how my Dad courted my mon in total purity and holiness, you would not even ask that question. You see, I was raised to understand that our Father in Heaven has designed one man and one woman matches over and over again. It's only when we, as mere mortals mess up the Father's plan that things get totally messed up. You see, Abby, I don't know if you are dating someone or understand what building a relationship the way the God the Father planned is all about. But this I do know. It's about time you found out."

Abby stepped back. "What are you, some sort of goodie two shoes which does not want to enjoy life?"

"Nope, I want to enjoy life God's way. We were all created for God's purpose, not for our baser wants. When two people love and respect each other, they do not want to enjoy the passions of a fleeting sexual drive for a few moments. It's when a couple loves each other enough and is willing to make a commitment for life that, I think, things would get the hottest. I have seen the clip of my mom and dad right after their honeymoon. Dad came back and pitched a perfect game. When the press asked mom some questions about their wedding night, she told them pitching is not the only thing he does perfectly."

Abby's face started to turn red just a bit. "You are for real; you really aren't out to take advantage of any women you date. You are for real!?" Abby stated.

Herman just smiled and winked at Abby. "Dinner then?" He asked.

"Where?" She asked.

"Justin's on the beach," Herman repeated. "Tomorrow at 7?" He asked.

Abby blushed. "Mr. McBrien, I would love to be there at 7.

Herman arrived first. He was sitting at the table overlooking lake Calhoun, in Mpls. Herman rose from his seat when Abby walked in and helped Abby with hers. Once seated, Abby started to ask the questions.

"Herman, what drives you, what, at this point in your career, makes you one of the greatest quarterbacks ever to step onto a football field?

Herman smiled. "Jesus." That was all he had to say.

Abby got a quizzical look on her face. "What do you mean?" She asked.

"Abby, you are a writer, correct?"

Abby smiled. "I like to think so." She answered.

"Where did your ability to write come from?" Herman asked.

Abby tilted her head. "I guess I was born with it."

Herman smiled. "You were designed with it. It was built into your DNA." He answered.

"What's your point?" She retorted.

"Abby, it's like this, God the Father through His Son Jesus by His Holy Spirit started planning us centuries ago. When we think of what our Father does to create each of us, we must remember that non-of-us are created on a whim. Abby, The Father, needed an Abby at this point in time. He created you. I don't know where your ancestors are from. But he had to move your ancestors from one part of the world to meet here in the states. He had to have our Fathers and Mothers meet to set up what he had in mind to draw more people to himself. For instance. My grandpa was living in Gotland, Sweden. My Grandma was living in Oklahoma. He had to have them meet to build my Mom. The Father had my grandpa meet my grandma in Chicago. Then he had to have my mom meet my dad in Neillsville, Wisconsin. All that was so my brother and sisters and myself could be born. "Herman said.

Abby smiled. "You think God plans each of us to that degree?"

Herman could not help but smile. "Abby, let me tell you this. Your single? Right."

"That is correct." She answered.

"Do you realize that our Father in Heaven has plans for your ancestor's centuries out from now?"

"Man, I did not." Was her answer.

"How do I meet the man that God has planned for me?" she asked, smiling at Herman.

- * -

The smile on the Father was wide as the ocean. "Pete, another success. You see how I am building intense feelings between the two. Neither one can deny the attraction that I am building between them. Herman is going to follow the tradition of his Dad, Eli. He will treat her like the present that I am having wrapped up for their wedding. You thought I gave Eli a reward for waiting; just wait with these two."

Peter smiled. He did not know exactly what the Father had in mind. But he knew it would be good.

The Father called Gabriel. "Hey, Gabe, get thumbnail front and center. I have another assignment for the little guy."

"You need me, sir? I love serving you; I really enjoyed what you had me doing on my last couple of assignments!" Thumbnail stated with pure joy.

"Little buddy, remember how I had you on Eli's shoulder. He could almost hear your breath. That's how close I want you to Herman."

Thumbnail could not help but smile.

- * -

Herman smiled. "You may have just met him."

Just then, Tommy and Kate and Jon and Jon's little brother Sammy walked up to them. The baby bump Kate was starting to show was getting obvious. Herman could not help but smile. "Tommy and Kate, look like your expanding your heritage a bit as well."

Tommy smiled instantly. "It's not just our heritage that we are expanding; it's also Jon's dad as well."

"What do you mean, Jon's dad, isn't that you?"

"Tommy looked directly at Herman intensely. "Herman, it's like this. Jon's dad was killed fighting for this country. Jon's last name is Goldsmith. His dad's heritage will be raised up by his son Jonathon." Sam and his little sister will raise up the heritage for Katie and I." Tommy said. We are committed to raising them in fear of God the Father through His Son Jesus by His Holy Spirit. I think what the Lord will do with them will be something amazing to see.

But my friend, we have something pressing coming up shortly, We play Chicago Sunday, It's our second to the last game of the season. We are in the playoffs. If we take out Chicago and Green Bay, we will have home field throughout the playoffs."

_ * _

The Father looked at Pete. "Peter, these two have worked all of their careers to come to this point. I know I am going to get the credit for their wins. Those wins they will achieve are going to surprise a lot of people. This is going to be fun." The Father said, smiling.

_ * _

All the players on Minnesota's team poured their hearts into the preparation for the last two games of the regular season. Both the players and coaches had the understanding that they may not ever get back to the level of perfection they were accomplishing this season. They reasoned together, as a team, that they had to achieve as close to perfection as humanly possible.

I am about to take a scripture out of context. In Matthew 5:46, Jesus ends a message on love with this statement: Be ye perfect as your Father in Heaven is perfect. At Saturday's evening chapel service, the team Chaplin stepped forward to give a short devotion before the team would board the plane and fly to Chicago. Jesus was talking about perfection in love. He was talking about loving those who it would be really tough to love. If God the Father can give us the ability to love those who are not lovable, giving us one or two perfect football games should be a piece of cake for him.

The next day they would go to the stadium especially early. Tommy and Herman would walk out onto the stadium floor just to "be" there. They walked to the 50-yard line. Looked to the right and left and just drank in the atmosphere of the Stadium.

Herman spoke first. "Tommy, think of all the years we have put in so we could play this one season together. Man, I really want the Super Bowl, not just to play in it, but win it all. I feel like we have this one shot at making a lifetime of football worth it."

Tommy smiled. "It's like this, bro; just get the ball to me; I will score a bunch of touchdowns; when our defense plays like we know they can, we have a shot. The one thing we really need to do right now is to pray."

As people were coming into the stadium, they could see Tommy and Herman kneeling in prayer in the middle of the stadium. The men in the broadcast booth had mixed emotions. John Paul, the lead broadcaster, said it well. "These men have poured their lives into this sport. I have known Tommy Henderson for years. I also know the story behind Herman McBrien. These two have one especially important thing in common. They both are alive today because of one woman. Jill McBrien. She gave birth to Herman, giving life to Tommy through a bone marrow transplant. These two men have wanted to play together for years. Tommy may have lost a step, but his experience and his still blazing speed make him a really tough cover. Herman's dad Eli was one of the greatest pitchers ever to step on the mound. His control was phenomenal. Herman seems to have that with a football. They look at their being able to play together for even one year as a miracle from God himself. Let's not criticize them, but let's go along for the ride and see what happens.

"Father, I know it may not be sportsman like to ask for a victory. I will ask that you have us play beyond our ability these next few games. We will give you the glory for every touchdown and field goal scored. In Jesus Name, please."

- * -

The Father looked at His Son Jesus and smiled. "Pete, call Charlie front and center. I have a big assignment for the Little Guy."

The rustling in the angel's quarters could not be hidden. It seemed that whenever Charlie got an assignment from the Highest, the Great I Am, all the angels in heaven started to get extremely excited. Charlie came flying out of his quarters to receive The Father's assignment.

"Father, what is it you want me to accomplish?" Thumbnail asked the Father.

The great I Am looked at his tiniest servant. "Thumbnail, I am going to use you to give these guys the best chance of winning, just like I do with all of my servants. You will be bouncing between Herman and Tommy and the coaches during the game. I will tell you what will work in any given situation. You will pass it on to the coaches, who will pass it on to the men on the field. It's still up to them to carry out their assignments. They will see success if they do their part and execute the plays that I call. You see, football is much like life. When I put football in the mind of Walter Camp, I had it in mind that the young men who would play this game would learn some very valuable life lessons. One of those lessons is to carry out my game plan and execute the plays I set up. If they do that, they will see victories and lives saved by the sacrifice my Son Jesus made on the cross. But they must follow the game plan, and they will see my victories. The Father looked at His littlest angel and said. "Let's go to work, little buddy!"

_*_

As the two of them prayed in the middle of the field, they could hear the jeers coming from the stands. Tommy prayed. "Father, you hear those guys making fun of us because we are invoking your name and asking for your protection as we play this game today. Father, I am going to be bold as I ask this. Father, don't just give us the win here today. I pray for a blowout. One in which we can stand together at the press conference and give the credit and glory to you, please. In Jesus Name, Amen."

_*_

The Father in Heaven was chuckling. He looked at His Son Jesus with The Holy Spirit as Thumbnail hovered nearby. "I have a score so big in my mind that no one has seen it before or will see it again. After the game, my men, Herman and Tommy, will stand mid-field and extol my glory over the win that I am going to give them. This is going to be so much fun!" The Father said.

_*_

The National Anthem was sung. Michelle Goldsmith sang a beautiful rendition of the Star-Spangled Banner. The teams stood at attention. The coin was tossed. Minnesota won the toss and elected to receive. As Herman walked to the coach. "Coach, I know you said we were going to use a run play to start the game. But what do you think of this? 49 power right fly. Let's use Tommy this game wide open from the get-go."

Coach Wolf could not help but smile. "Great idea, let' make it work."

Herman ran into the huddle. "49 power right fly. Let's light this field on fire. Break!"

The huddle broke. Tommy lined up on the right, Johnson lined up on the left. Both receivers flew down the field. Herman would hit Johnson in the hands for the first of many touchdowns in that game. The final score would be 77-3. Johnson would catch 3 touchdown passes. Run for another, Tommy would catch three, and the defense would intercept one and return it for a touchdown. One punt return for another touchdown. Johnson would score 2 for a total of 10 touchdowns.

After the game, Tommy and Herman were standing together at the podium.

A sweet young reporter from Chicago daily asked a question. "I saw you two gentlemen kneeling and praying before the game. Do you feel there was some 'divine intervention' with this game?"

Tommy spoke up. "Young lady, did you hear the ridicule we took for praying before the game?" Beth, the young reporter, answered. "Yes, I did."

Tommy then answered her question. "In Galatians 6:7, Paul writes. "God is not mocked; a man shall reap what he sows' It Seems to me you folks from Chicago thought our praying was a waste of time. Our Father in Heaven through His Son Jesus by His Holy Spirit had it in their mind to show up and show off. And so, he did."

- * -

Thumbnail jumped up and down in the Father's presence. "Father, thank you for using me in this game; it was so much fun."

The Father smiled. "Sometimes, my little buddy, we just gotta teach those who doubt me not to. You did well, good and faithful servant."

Green bay would not be as easy a game. Minnesota could squeak out a victory, and they were headed for the playoffs.

17. SUPERBOWL HERE WE COME

Having secured home-field advantage throughout the playoffs and a bye for the first week, both Tommy and Herman were able to be at home with their loved ones for the first week of the playoffs. Tommy and Herman watched St. Louis play L.A. As they watched the defense of both teams, Abby and Beth in the other room were listening to them naming plays that they could use against the defenses that were being used against the offenses of both teams.

Abby looked over at Beth. "Beth, you cover these sports. Do you understand the language those two guys in the other room are using?"

Beth could only smile. "Not a clue." That was all she could say.

Practice the following Monday would be one of watching St. Louis's win over L.A. The offensive squad would watch St. Louis's defense and defense of St Louis's offense. One could almost hear the clicking of the synoptic connections in all the player's brains as they were totally engrossed in watching the team that would be standing in their way of getting to and finally winning the Superbowl.

Practice that week would be brutal. The guys on the practice squad would get hit so hard their heads were ringing all the way home. Minnesota's game plan was set. Both offense and defense had their game plan set. Nothing was going to come between them and their goal of victory.

Sunday's game against St. Louis would turn to be a brutal match-up. The game would turn out to be much closer than Minnesota wanted it to be. The margin of victory would be only one point. As they walked into the locker room, the coach stepped up on the bench. "Gentlemen, a win is a win, is a win, is a win. Take your wives and significant others to dinner tomorrow. We get ready for Tampa. Let's get this next win under put under our ` belt. Then we will know who our opponent in the Bowl will be."

Tommy called Kate, and Herman called Beth. Tommy and Kate's boys would be joining them for dinner. When Tommy and Kate sat down, the look on Jon's face was one of instant infatuation.

"Ms. Beth, I think I have seen you somewhere before? Are you a T.V. star?" Jon asked, a bit red in the face.

"Jon, I don't know if I would call myself a star; I am a reporter for K.D.Z, Y television. I am a sports reporter. I really don't know if that would make me famous."

"You do know my dad here is famous, don't you?" Jon asked Beth.

Beth could not help but smile. "If you bring up your dad's name in any house in the country, they will know who you are talking about, that is for sure."

Then Jon leaned across the table. "Miss Beth, you do know my last name is not Richardson, don't you?"

Beth got a puzzled look on her face. "What do you mean?"

"It's like this. My dad was killed before I was born. God brought my mom and Tommy together. One night, not too long ago, God let my dad come back and sit beside my bed. The glow was bright. It woke me up. My real dad and I talked for a long time. I sat on his lap. He told me I could trust Tommy. It was amazing."

Beth was now even more puzzled. She looked over at Kate and quietly asked her. "He was dreaming, right?"

Kate knew she had to tell the truth. In her deepest being, she had wished Jon had not brought up when he had sat on his dad's lap. But she knew she could not lie about what she saw. "No, Beth, he was not dreaming. It was late at night. I was walking past his room. I saw the bright light shining through every crack in his door. I opened it slightly and saw him sitting on his daddy's lap. He had his arms around his son like he would never let him go. I heard this voice; I don't know if it was Jesus, God, the Holy Spirit, or an Angel. It told me to step back, close the door quietly. This was a Holy time for them both. It was the only time that they would have together until Jon would meet his dad in heaven."

Beth got a puzzled look on her face. "For real? Does anyone else know about this?" She asked.

"No one, and it had better stay that way if you get my drift."

Beth got close to Kate. "Some stories need to be told; some stories can't be. This one can't be. I have never heard of that sort of thing happening, but this I do know, with God, all things are possible."

Kate smiled. I do know this. This is one experience that he will have that he will carry for the rest of his life. After that experience, he will never doubt Jesus and the Father through the Holy Spirit for the rest of his life.

At that second, the phone rang. Kate picked up the phone. On the other end was Tommy. "Sweetheart, we play the Montana Bison for the RFC. CHAMPIONSHIP. After that, the big game. Pray, we can keep our focus on what it needs to be.

Kate felt two emotions. One total excitement that the man the Father through the Son by the Spirit brought into her and Jon's life was about to accomplish his greatest goal, and the second was that a lifelong connection with his "brother" was about to be cemented even deeper by the touchdown passes that Herman would be throwing.

As the team walked into the field house the Monday before the big game, they saw Coach Wolf with a big smile on his face. He handed each of the players on offense over to the sideline.

"Gentlemen, we are about to do something that has never been done in Minnesota. We are going to win the Superbowl. We play Cleveland, who has had an amazing year. It will be our toughest game of the year, as it should be. What we must keep in mind is this. We are here to bring home a win. We are here to bring Glory to the Father of all mankind. The king of kings, the great I Am."

Herman looked at his coach. "What's the path to victory, coach?" He asked.

Coach Wolf would say. "This week, the defense is going to be going over every formation and play they have ever run. This week, we will work on a play that could win the game for us if we need it. The key to victory could come down to one play at the end of the game. Gentlemen, let's go to work." With that, the players went to their warm-ups. Coach wolf had been in touch with his high school football coach, Jim Erickson. He had him send over a play they used only once.

He had it in mind just in case the game was on the line, and they had one shot for a win. It would be used only once in the game.

The team went over and over the play. Herman walked up to coach wolf and asked him if he could do something a bit out of the ordinary when it came time to call out the signals at the line of scrimmage on that one play. Permission was granted.

The teams would be working their behinds off getting ready for the game. Both Cleveland and Minnesota knew what was at stake. They realized the Super bowl team members' winner was looking at some huge endorsement contracts because of that win. The fact of the matter went back to Tommy having made a promise to himself. He just wanted to offer his Superbowl ring to Jill for saving his life when he was diagnosed with Leukemia at age 10. Tommy had made enough money to last him the rest of his life. That life he was looking forward to, in large part, was because of Jill's willingness to give him the life that the Father had planned for him before time began.

_*_

"Pete, watch this. They will use a play that I put into Jim Erickson's mind years ago. The play was only used once. The one time it was used completely blew away Milaca, who Carlton was playing for the state championship. The Father was smiling a smile as wide as the Grande Canyon.

_*_

As they walked on the field against Cleveland, they were ready. They had spent all season working for this one game. Every day the silent goal was to beat the team they were playing to be ready for the final conclusion. Both Herman and Tommy knew there would be no tomorrow for them. They both wanted to be able to say to their kids as they grew that the "brothers" had accomplished something great by working with the rest of their team to accomplish that which the Father, through the Son by the Spirit, had created them for. This would be their crowning game. Herman would have several years left to play. He would play each game with a huge passion, but non with his passion with this one.

The game score see-sawed back and forth. It came down to the last few seconds of the game. Minnesota was down by 4, so a field goal did them no good. They had 40 yards to go. They had practiced this play and had it down to a T.

Herman walked into the huddle. He looked over at his big tackle, who had shown his prowess for throwing the pass he would be required to throw to Tommy all season. Herman smiled as he looked at the giant of a man. Its time was all he had to say to him. Herman looked around the huddle. Gentlemen, payday on 2.

"Kyle, we are sitting here with two seconds left on the clock. Minnesota is trailing by 4 points. A field goal does them no good. Their coach Dennis Wolf has something up his sleeve. He has made calls all season long that have made his team shine. But what could he possibly do? have in mind now?"

"Tim, look over at the sidelines. There is something you don't see very often. Both McBrien and Tommy Henderson are huddled with the coach on the sidelines. They are cooking up something, but I don't know what's going on. If you check out the skybox, you will see Tommy's mom Janice and Eli, and Jill McBrien talking about what could be up to their sleeve as well. Do you have any clue what could be possible in the works?"

Tim replied. "Kyle, they seem to be praying. I know that both families have a deep faith in Christ, and they depend on him for everything. But prayer for a football game? Sure, this is the Super Bowl, but prayer for a football game?"

Tommy looked intently at Coach Wolf. "Coach, what your calling here is the play. If it works, you are a hero for having the guts to call it. But..."

Coach Wolf looked intently into the faces of his two players as he said. "This play has to be something they have no clue is coming. They know every play in our book. The two of us have one thing in common. We both played our high school ball under Jim Erickson. Just at different times. We have everything against us here. When it comes to the last play, who do you trust?"

Herman looked directly into Wolf's eyes. "I trust God our Father. And I know exactly what I am going to say when we get to the line." He said with an intensity in his voice that surprised even him.

Wolf looked at his men and only had one thing left to say. "Get 'er done!" Both men headed back to the huddle.

The two men reached the huddle. The clock would start running at the snap of the ball. Herman barked out the signals. "Power right, 26 crash sweeps left. Pass left 36 crosses 25 fly. On 2. Break!"

Both teams lined up on the ball. Eli bent down under center and started to bark out the signals. "35,22, Not by might, not by power, but by my spirit, says the Lord." The whole Cleveland team looked up. Herman yelled, "Go"!

Tommy took a step back and ran behind Eli, who flipped the ball. Looking like he still had it; he sprinted right like he was going to throw down to Bruce Johnson, his fullback. Johnson cut sharply to the sideline. They had him covered tightly as he had been giving them fits all day.

Herman cut up field then turned on the afterburners and Tommy set and made a perfect throw. The ball would drop into his arms Herman's arms like a loaf of bread. Finally, Minnesota had its ultimate victory.

The two men stood beside each other on the podium in the middle of the field. They basked in the screams and adulation of the 900000 fans still in the stand. Tim Johnson, the league commissioner, stood between Tommy and Herman. "Gentlemen, do you have anything to say to your fans who just watched you with that final play that put Minnesota in the win column for the Superbowl?

Tommy and Herman looked at each other; both knew what they wanted to say. Tommy looked at Herman and said. " I have had a great career, folks. After this, there is nothing left to win for me in this game. And folks, let's be real. That's all it is; it's a game. From here, I will dedicate the rest of my life to serving the Lord Jesus Christ. Let me take this opportunity to ask you each a question."

"You have each enjoyed a game with a lot of excitement. You have each seen men who have poured their whole life into a game to achieve as much as they possibly could in that game. God The Father has allowed me to play the game I loved for many years. But if it weren't for an absolute miracle when I was a young lad and Herman's mother donating bone marrow, I would not even be here. I am going to take this opportunity to ask you each a question. Where are you with God the Father through His Son Jesus by His Holy Spirit? Have you surrendered to the Lordship of Jesus Christ? Can I see a show of hands of the people here who want to receive Christ as their savior tonight? Will you pray with me to receive Christ?"

At least 20000 hands went up around the stadium. Tommy stepped forward just a bit and led everyone in a prayer to receive Christ. After the game, Tommy formalized his retirement. He would spend the rest of his life with his bride and their children helping people build their relationships with Christ.

Now is the time if you have not received Christ as your personal lord and Savior. There is nothing more important in your life than having that intimate personal relationship with Christ.

EPILOGUE

This is the last of the Eli Series. These books have been a labor of love. I pray that Jesus has shown himself to you through these books in a way that will upbuild you for years to come. I Pray God's richest Blessing on you.

- Michael D. Goldsmith

Made in the USA
Monee, IL
03 July 2023